Let Me Finish.

Let Me Finish.

Udo Grashoff

headline
review

Copyright © Reclam Verlag Leipzig 2004

The right of Udo Grashoff to be identified as the Author
of the Work has been asserted by him in accordance with the
Copyright, Designs and Patents Act 1988.

First published in 2004 by
Reclam Verlag Leipzig

First published in Great Britain in 2006
by Headline Review
An imprint of Headline Book Publishing

2

ISBN 0 7553 1443 3

Cataloguing in Publication Data is available
from the British Library

Typeset by Palimpsest Book Production Limited,
Polmont, Stirlingshire

Printed and bound in Great Britain by
Antony Rowe Ltd, Chippenham, Wiltshire

Headline's policy is to use papers that are natural, renewable
and recyclable products and made from wood grown in sustainable forests.
The logging and manufacturing processes are expected to conform to the
environmental regulations of the country of origin.

HEADLINE BOOK PUBLISHING
A division of Hodder Headline
338 Euston Road
London NW1 3BH

Every effort has been made to fulfil requirements with regard
to reproducing copyright material. The author and publisher will be glad
to rectify any omissions at the earliest opportunity.

www.headline.co.uk
www.hodderheadline.com

Contents

Introduction

Why Write This Book?

"'Kill yourself? – What's the point? It achieves absolutely nothing." Precisely: it achieves nothing, and nothingness is what I want.' These words – written by the Austrian poet Herta Kräftner in her diary in September 1951, two months before she killed herself – have a determined, self-assured ring. But why did the twenty-three-year-old crave 'nothingness'?

An engineer, who killed his whole family as well as himself, wrote a crowing PS at the end of his suicide letter: 'We're happier than you are'. To those (like me) who wish to carry on living and who believe that the future holds endless opportunities, such words are hard to understand. What can possibly have so warped someone's vision and so utterly destroyed their hopes that they long for death and actively seek it? In earlier centuries the Church offered a simple answer to comfort those left behind: anyone who killed himself was 'possessed by the Devil'. In the present day medicine appears to offer an explanation: suicide is seen as the conclusion of a pathological process.

Medical explanations may be valid in many cases, but not everyone who takes their own life is ill. Suicide is not brought about by a syndrome of some kind. This has been pointed out more than once by the writer and commentator Jean Améry, among others. Suicide is one of mankind's privileges, an option available to everyone.

Children seldom seek death, probably because they have no realistic concept of what it means to 'do away with yourself', but it is a possibility that begins to take shape during puberty at the latest. Psychiatrists agree that, in principle, there is potential risk of a suicide attempt in every young person passing through adolescence. We live our lives knowing that we are free to end them; but how do we deal with this knowledge?

Even today, suicide is a subject that people prefer not to talk about. Cases of suicide can trigger intense fear, especially in those who are closely involved with the person, such as spouses, friends and even therapists. As psychoanalysts often stress, people's own fear of death is activated by encounters with the suicidal tendencies of others. This fear probably also lies at the heart of the suicide taboo.

The unspoken rule forbidding open discussion of suicide was maintained for centuries in the West, particularly by the Church. According to Christian doctrine, those who took their own lives were putting themselves beyond the moral pale and were almost seen as criminals. Since the eighteenth-century Enlightenment, the taboo has increasingly lost its force, but its after-effects are still perceptible. We retain a blend of fear and fascination that has impeded both our ability to understand suicide and our capacity to find an appropriate way of dealing with it.

Within the Christian churches, a less simplistic approach to suicide, owing a great deal to the insights of modern medicine, has gained ascendancy. In the media, the topic of suicide is now generally presented and discussed in a factual way. This book likewise seeks to offer a dispassionate perspective on suicide – avoiding the current trench warfare over such politicised issues as assisted suicide and attempted suicide. I believe that we should look calmly at this subject, instead of either staring or averting our eyes as we have done in the past. In my view, our society needs to take stock not only of success, but also of failure, as we see amongst us every day.

Now that suicide is the subject of professional interest and analytical debate, the death of people by their own hands is sometimes interpreted in totally distorted ways. Doctors hunt for risk factors that predispose people to suicide, and – in line with the principles of preventive medicine – seek to devise protective measures. Sociologists generalise on the basis of individual cases and link suicide rates to the weather, the economy, the political situation or even 'happiness'. Moral theologians methodically weigh up different ethical factors in order to discover whether or not there are worse evils than suicide. Journalists exploit the cliché of the 'victim driven to suicide' in order to criticise institutions they don't like.

Novelists use the motif of suicide to depict unusually self-obsessed tragic heroes.

My own activities also need to be included in this list, as I have been working for several years on a contemporary history dissertation, analysing the way suicide was dealt with in the former East Germany, the German Democratic Republic (GDR). I am often asked what caused me, as a historian, to devote my energies to the topic of suicide. Reasons that one might expect, such as suicide attempts of my own – the reason given by Al Alvarez, for instance, author of *The Savage God*, for his interest in suicide – do not apply in my case, and there have been no traumatic deaths among my family or friends. What led me to the taboo subject of suicide was my search for a research topic with an 'existential' dimension, and one that has so far been little explored. As I combed through the documentation in various archives, I came across numerous suicide letters that I found very striking and often deeply moving. The idea then arose that I should publish some of these letters in book form.

The original documents consisted mainly of photocopies and transcripts from the archives of the police, security services, education authorities, medical publications and medical dissertations, and some have already been published in books and magazines. Spelling mistakes and grammatical errors have been left unchanged so that the letters appear exactly as they did in the originals.

To safeguard the privacy of surviving family members, dates, places and other details (such as family relationships and number of children) have been altered or deleted. Names have been replaced by initials. The letters therefore make it possible to share in authentic testaments to human despair without the issue being clouded by specific personalities. No one social class has a monopoly on suicide: education, intelligence and social position have almost no effect on the likelihood of any particular individual committing suicide. Furthermore, suicide letters by artists and other prominent figures, and suicide letters from the world of literature, have already been published elsewhere, and could therefore be largely dispensed with in the present book.

The Logic of Failure

Can suicide letters contribute to a better understanding of people who die by their own hand? W. Morgenthaler, a Swiss psychologist who embarked on an analysis of suicide letters some sixty years ago, remarked that 'severe disappointment awaits anyone inclined to expect that people who have decided to take leave of life and stand before the dark gates of death become especially clear-sighted, or can offer us a better slant on the mysteries of death and dying, or can even peer through the gates into the realm beyond. Quite the reverse is true: their gaze becomes not clearer but more befuddled, or at the very least severely restricted.'

Suicide letters bear witness to their writers' final hours, and as such they give insight into that person's emotions and thought processes in the period immediately prior to death. What is revealing in such letters is not only *what* is said, but also the *manner* in which it is said. Profound utterances and blatant banalities often jostle against one another, making the letters seem grotesque and sometimes even unintentionally comic. Everything is expressed in abstract terms; such detail as exists is confined chiefly to instructions regarding the person's accounts. Their explanations of their reasons for killing themselves are often vague and incomplete, and some-times false. Morgenthaler found that motives were falsely stated in sixteen out of forty-four letters – in three cases, surprisingly enough, to the disadvantage of the writer. In another analysis, of eighty-three different instances, eleven were found to be untrue and twenty only partly true. The great majority, however, fifty-two out of the eighty-three, did prove to be accurate.

But even when people try to offer a sincere and genuine explanation, doubts remain whether it is ever possible to express the real truth of the matter. 'I've spent ages wondering whether I should write or not. And that's because the more you think about it, the more difficult it is to maintain any hope of ever being understood.' This is how a father begins a lengthy suicide letter in which he tries to make clear that 'something inside me has snapped; something that won't ever grow back together again.' The man describes his experience of mental illness (including electric-shock therapy), his slide down the social ladder, his increasing isolation – an account that we can empathise with, in spite or even because of, its exaggerations.

The people talking in these letters are close to death; they themselves are doing the talking; and they are talking for the last time. Reading their suicide letters means accompanying them on part of their final journey; it means listening to words that they have addressed to someone we know nothing about and never see. In their final lines people no longer tell the full story or try to get to the bottom of things or spell them out in great detail: they offer their final pronouncements. The letters – often written in haste – are like a flurry of blows, some light, some heavy, many of them not particularly well aimed.

My original intention was to collect these frequently gloomy, sometimes stumbling, yet forceful letters into a book and publish them as they are, with the barest of commentaries. I wanted to release the letters from the analytical embrace of sociologists, philosophers, doctors and lawyers, for – in their calm conceptual world – extreme distress and utter failure tend to melt away and become mere abstractions. I wanted to lay bare the pain and show how, *in extremis*, language failed these people who felt themselves like failures. In the course of working on the manuscript, however, I realised how important it was to provide information on the context, the background, the letter's addressee and – last but not least – the deed itself. Each of the letters is therefore followed by a commentary containing all the important pieces of available inform-ation. This information largely comes from police records, and is limited by their scope.

The Traumatic Effects of Suicide on Other People

'A man who retires from life does no harm to society,' wrote the Scottish philosopher David Hume in his famous essay in defence of suicide. On this point he was wrong, although the after-effects of suicide have only recently begun to receive consideration. For many people, the suicide of a family member has the impact of a terrorist act. It causes the abrupt and violent rupture of social relationships and can cause feelings of guilt in relatives. Spouses, parents, children, friends or colleagues of the person may imagine that they, too, can feel the pull of death – a burden that can weigh on them for many years.

Most people writing suicide letters appear to realise that their decision will affect family members and friends. Depending on their motivation, they either deliberately set out to create feelings of guilt and pangs of conscience, or else they apologise in advance for the heavy burden they are imposing on others.

An abandoned wife writes to her rival: 'I just hope you've got enough of a conscience to see that *you* are to blame for what I'm doing. I hope your marriage to my husband produces at least five children!'

Such curses are rare. They are most commonly found among the small number of suicides who take other people with them. The final letter of a multiple murderer, for instance, ends with violent attacks on three further individuals: 'I'm letting them live in the hope that they will die a long and painful death.' More often than not, such attacks are half-stifled, broken off almost before they have begun, as in the case of the schoolgirl who expressed her feelings: 'Dear parents, [. . .] It's not right for you to know that I hate you, but I don't want to cause you any more worry.'

The dominant feature in most letters is an intense desire for harmony, forgiveness and reconciliation. 'If you can, then forget the bad times with me. Perhaps there were a few nice hours as well that you can think back on,' writes an abandoned husband to his wife.

A fifteen-year-old schoolboy, who hanged himself in his bedroom, also painted a somewhat ambivalent picture in his final lines. His parents had often run him down, calling him a 'slob' and a 'filthy pig'. In response to these accusations from his 'shitty family', he simply made a half-hearted attempt to set the record straight: 'okay, I agree that some of it was true, but not all of it.'

The mild tone of many letters is probably also due to the fact that the actual act of suicide itself conveys an aggressive message, whereas the suicide note is 'at most a form of confirmation', as the psychotherapist Bluma Lewinsky-Aurbach has quite rightly remarked. The written message is intended to round out the picture and justify the writer's actions; it is a final attempt to soften the dreadful image of someone about to hang himself or leap from a tall building, someone intent on 'dying by their own hand'.

A father, just turned fifty, imagines his family after his

death: 'I expect you are all very sad now. There you are sitting around the table, and there's an empty chair.' Then he adds: 'But that's only how it seems on the outside. I'm still there – in you and through you.'

In a spirit of paternal love, a businessman bestows a final blessing on his son: 'If there's any way I can watch over you from the other side, then I shall certainly do so.'

Writers of suicide letters often try to compensate for the negative effect they expect their death to produce. In a long and passionate letter, offering solace to his relatives, an Ethiopian student wrote: 'Support one another. Above all, don't forget my father and my brother. Comfort my father.'

These attempts at consolation frequently seem futile. When, for instance, two German youngsters, tired of life, told their parents that they had 'no reason to be sad' and should 'rejoice with us, for we are happy to have found this path to self-destruction', it seems more than likely their words had the opposite effect.

But then there is this, too: a man unhappy in love, who kills himself and tells his relatives that: 'It's thanks to you that I didn't do this any earlier.'

Signals from the Gates of Death

Suicide letters document the proximity of death, which has not – as yet – arrived. The letter-writers can therefore offer us no insights into the hereafter, but some do manage to convey how agonising and difficult their final hours are. 'Never thought dying would be so difficult,' notes one man, 'but I have to do it all the same.' A woman stresses that taking her own life 'disgusts' her. But dying is accepted as the lesser evil. 'At last I'm experiencing death, life was terrible,' writes a woman with the gas already pouring out.

Some are not altogether certain that they really want to die. 'By the time you get this letter I may already be dead, unless I'm in luck and manage to survive': so writes a young sailor to his parents before leaping into the freezing cold sea; he was known to be a strong swimmer, and he also donned a lifejacket. This ambivalent mood, in which people both want to die and also carry on living, is the rule rather than the exception. Around 80 per cent of those who survive an attempted suicide are glad to have done so and never repeat the attempt. This statistic is often quoted by doctors in order to justify the measures they take to revive such people – sometimes against their will. The majority of those who attempt to end their lives don't necessarily want to die. Above all, they wish to break a cycle, to end an intolerable situation, or to seek help. Unfortunately, such a cry for help will only be taken seriously if the attempt at suicide is a serious one. The sad result of this need to knock on death's door is that many people die who actually wanted to be saved.

There is also a smaller group whose suicide can be delayed by medical intervention, but not prevented. This book therefore includes not only documents testifying to inner turmoil and uncertainty, but also letters that express definite resolve. A pensioner suffering from persecution mania ended her almost incomprehensible letter with the uncompromising remark that 'I had no influence on the beginning of my life, but I *am* going to have an influence on its end.' Prior to this, she had called the police on several occasions because of alleged 'damage to property within her dwelling caused by persons unknown', and complained of damage that didn't actually exist. Haunted and humiliated by her fantasies of persecution, she appears to have been able to achieve clarity of mind only by this means. In killing herself, she wanted to see herself for one last time as someone controlling her own actions.

Suicide letters not only document their writers' struggles with death, but often also demonstrate attempts to think ahead to what awaits them *after* death. Suicide researchers are all agreed that the purpose of these death fantasies is to lower the individual's own instinctive resistance to suicide and to justify and reinforce their decision to end their life. At the same time they are also an attempt to fill the vacuum that in previous centuries was filled by religion.

In the past, Christianity gave the afterlife a specific structure and projected a pattern of Good and Evil onto it. The Church's prohibition against suicide was a threat that probably did sometimes stop people killing themselves. However, those who were quite determined to die could scarcely expect kind treatment in the afterlife anyway. They therefore faced the same problem as atheists: they had to use their own imaginations to summon up a vision of what it would be like once they were dead. With fewer people practising Christianity nowadays more people face this problem, as shown in the letters in this book. These lonely attempts to give some kind of meaning to their actions appear in numerous suicide letters. In many cases their writers try to construct a world view that makes sense of their own paradoxical act of self-destruction/self-liberation.

Two youths, for instance, create a vision of an eternal and spiritual humanity: 'We shall live on in people's dreams, in their sorrows and fears, in their goodness and their badness, in justice and injustice, in the strong and the weak. As erstwhile true human beings [. . .] we shall live for ever in the rest of humanity.' Although both young-sters grew up in Christian families, they latched onto the Buddhist notion of the transmigration of souls and – in their longing for reassurance about the hereafter – resorted to a religion that has a relatively relaxed attitude to suicide.

Like this letter, many others also reveal a determina-tion to smooth out the difference between life and death. In some cases, though, this approach to death has its roots in psychotic delusions. In a letter of several pages an engineer sought to prove the necessity of his death by reference to thermodynamics and its laws of equilibrium. He defined the world as a closed system whose compo-nent parts annihilate one another – and he, the writer, knew the only way out: 'Either you set everything aside and follow me, or you are done for. That is my message to you.'

A prison inmate – a suspected psychotic given to talking

to the objects in his cell – wrote to his family: 'I want to become 100 per cent an object, instead of always being neither this nor that, just something in between. I've talked it all through with the objects here and they tell me it's not before time.'

In some suicide fantasies, music serves as a link between the world of the dead and the world of the living. A woman who killed herself in her uncle's flat after a marital row begged him to 'play a Beethoven sonata once you have read this letter, the Moonlight perhaps, and think for a moment how much I liked hearing you play'. And a fifteen-year-old schoolboy hopes that 'Eleanor Rigby', the Beatles song, will help his schoolmates to understand his suicide: he wants them to listen to the song after his death because it 'talks about my problems too'.

Quite often the letters contain instructions about the funeral or the kind of grave the person wants. The two German teenagers mentioned earlier asked for a 'cheap burial without much palaver', and without flowers or death announcements, and added that 'the money saved could be better spent on a donation' to the German charity Bread for the World.

'Dear L,' writes a young man, just before shooting himself, 'please ask my mother to put the garden gnome on my grave.'

Other letter-writers specify what is to be done with their mortal remains. Alongside utterances such as 'I am to be burnt' or 'bury me like a dog', we also find attempts to prevent a post mortem. Thus a doctor described her own cause of death in minute detail in order to make an autopsy unnecessary.

Going Backwards into Death

There is an above-average frequency of the word 'love' in suicide letters. This is not very surprising, as most such letters are addressed to their writers' nearest and dearest. 'I love you like I've never loved anyone before,' writes a lovelorn prison inmate to a fellow prisoner before hanging himself.

Love is presented in many letters as an object of longing, something that was either never achieved or now lies in tatters – and it is often evoked with an undertone of reproach. Therefore a husband tells his wife, who is seeking a divorce: 'Maybe if you'd been a bit more affectionate and tender (at any rate recently), it would never have come to this. I don't know. I know only that it's something I absolutely longed for.'

Another young man tells his beloved that 'you mean more to me than you can ever imagine. [. . .] I love you, and the thought of this makes the step I'm taking a little bit easier, because I can't fight for your love – that's an option you never allowed me.'

When people are on the point of killing themselves, and are filled with despair and disappointment, they can also feel – or imagine that they feel – an upsurge of the love that in real life has been irretrievably lost or destroyed. Those writing their farewell letters in such terms go to their deaths facing backwards. To the very last, their eyes are fixed on their lives, on the entanglements that seemed so insoluble to them, and that they now wish to eradicate at one fell swoop, as if cutting the Gordian knot.

In some cases, people's irrepressible compulsions can still be seen in their final acts. 'Please tell G I really loved him, he never understood me [. . .] The man lying next to me is just an unfortunate coincidence': thus writes a woman well known to the police for her multiple sexual liaisons. On the eve of her death she had taken yet another man home with her, then turned the gas tap on during the night – with the result that he, too, was gassed as he lay there asleep in blissful ignorance.

Some suicides, on the other hand, involve an 'act of love', such as when people follow their spouses or partners into death. Therefore a recently widowed woman recounts having met her dead husband in a dream; in a kind of serene twilight he had led her to other ghostly figures. 'You just can't imagine how relieved I feel now,' she told friends in whose company she had spent a lovely last day, before killing herself.

More Light?

The final words of artists and other famous people on their deathbeds – such as Goethe's 'More light!' – have encouraged the supposition that *anyone's* final words might carry more significance than all the countless moments of their entire previous life, and can be regarded as a kind of summing up of their whole existence.

In the case of suicide, the Christian Church's traditional stance of moral condemnation, and the efforts of various philosophers to counter this by reinterpreting suicide as an act of heroism, have encouraged us to emphasise the importance of this final act even more. These are some of the reasons why, even today, it is difficult to arrive at an appropriate attitude in the face of suicide.

Before killing herself, the Austrian poet Hertha Kräftner wrote in her diary: 'Time draws together like the drawstring on a bag; the bag hangs down, black as black, into empty space. Death is down there, and we fall into it.' Schoolchildren, students, housewives, engineers, doctors, lawyers, policemen and prison inmates do not always draw such a poetic line under their lives in their suicide notes.

If anyone, it is mainly the young who seek to transfigure their departure from life by making grave and grandiose utterances. Therefore the seventeen-year-olds mentioned earlier quote the Bible ('For here we have no continuing city, but we seek one to come') and offer portentous metaphors ('We felt as if we were on an escalator that was travelling the wrong way'). In so doing, they seek to turn their premature deaths into the emblematic story of an entire lost generation, whose 'souls have no home'.

Another seventeen-year-old prefaced his suicide letter with a poem, based on a well-known German song: 'No more joy, no more love, / No more sun or moon to see,

/ A little bit nasty: just a corpse. / Not very nice for you either, I reckon.'

In marked contrast to this is the extreme brevity of many older people, who often no longer bother to write whole letters but leave just a few words: 'My pain is terrible, I can't go on,' or 'I've been planning this for ages. You'll find me in the cellar,' or even just a curt 'Goodbye'.

Suicide as a Mass Phenomenon

As society modernised, official records began being kept of the number of people committing suicide. Although a considerable number of suicides remain undetected (around 25 per cent, according to researchers), the collection and publication of suicide statistics do allow us to assess the scale of the phenomenon.

The figures show that suicide is far from being a minor issue. Suicides are in fact more frequent than other causes of death that attract much discussion. For instance, in England and Wales in 2004, 6,121 deaths were on the roads and 190 deaths were from AIDS – while Samaritans' figures for the last decade show annual deaths by suicide (including undetermined deaths) to be between 5,000 and 7,000 each year. In Western Europe, suicide statistics were already available in the first half of the nineteenth century – and revealed that people were killing themselves in increasing numbers. Explanations were soon found, usually in support of particular critiques of society. The collapse of traditional social structures, secularisation, the weakening of family ties and the increasing isolation of city-dwellers were all cited as factors towards the increase in suicides. The suicide rate, that is to say the number of suicides per 100,000 inhabitants of a given area in a given year, therefore came to be regarded as a measure of the negative effects of modern living.

Although they were grinding a particular axe, such interpretations had a real basis in fact. Indeed, ever since the French sociologist Emile Durkheim published his seminal study in 1897, it has been universally accepted that family and religious ties lower the risk of suicide. One problem with Durkheim's study, though, is that he could only see an increase in suicide figures as a result of social disintegration, rather than a statistical figure.

The exploitation of suicide statistics is a lamentable tradition that has continued for a very long time – and not only by scandal-obsessed journalists. Suicide statistics have been used and abused as a political weapon in support of all manner of different political causes. Therefore, August Bebel based his social-democratic critique of German society partly on suicide figures for women. President Eisenhower used precisely the opposite argument: noting that suicide rates in Sweden were higher than in the USA, he blamed this on Sweden's socialist system. The former West Germany used similar arguments about the former East Germany, and it is characteristic of the East German communist regime's political methods that they ultimately put an end to the debate in 1963 by banning publication of their suicide statistics.

It is always dangerous to link suicide rates with a particular political or social system, since it means using the suicide rate – which hovers around 0·2 per 1,000 – as an indicator for the state of an entire society. Furthermore, such sweeping generalisations make no allowance for the huge number of different motives behind suicide. Saying that social deprivation, political repression or economic crises lead to an increase in the number of suicides is also open to debate. The opposite is often the case. But quite apart from politically motivated interpretations, *all* generalisations about suicide rates are risky, since they lump together a huge variety of different causes and intentions.

One interesting aspect of suicide rates, which is not easily explained, is the steady patterns revealed by the statistics, with some of the patterns remaining stable for decade after decade. For example, in both the UK and the US men commit suicide more often than women. Suicide rates also show seasonal fluctuations, the most popular months in the northern hemisphere being May and June (a fact some may find surprising) and in the southern hemisphere, November.

Statistical comparisons have helped to identify several other groups at particular risk of suicide, including alcoholics, drug addicts and the mentally ill. The risk also increases following divorce or the loss of loved ones. However, these are simply factors that tend to favour suicidal behaviour. Statistics on their own can tell us nothing about why particular individuals decide to take their own lives. We should therefore consider two other

approaches: one that sees suicide as the end of a pathological process, and another that views it as a specific
form of problem-solving behaviour.

Suicide as Illness

In recent decades, psychiatrists and psychologists have
chiefly concentrated on trying to find the *reasons* for any
increase in suicidal tendencies. A key aim of suicide
research is to use any knowledge gained to help calculate the suicide risk of particular patients.

To this end, medical research into suicide has devel-
oped many theories. In the process, purely psychiatric
explanations have lost ground. Only a small percentage
of people who kill themselves are mentally ill. And,
although psychiatric patients demonstrably present an
increased risk of suicide, their reasons – when they do
actually kill themselves – in most cases can be explained
in normal psychological terms. Often, the reasons centre
on a breakdown in personal relationships.

Older forms of diagnosis such as 'psychopathy' (implying
the notion of a fixed psychopathic personality) have been
replaced in recent decades by different approaches that
look for crises and problematic developments in people's
lives. In numerous patients psychotherapists have found
a form of behaviour that causes conflicts to escalate and
therefore leads almost inevitably to a suicidal crisis. Where
there is a so-called 'narcissistic personality disorder', which
originates in a dysfunctional mother-child relationship,

the individual's self-image oscillates between feelings of worthlessness and a grandiose but solitary sense of self-importance. When relationships break down, narcissistic personalities react in an extreme way, often attempting suicide because they find the situation so wounding as to be unbearable. In such cases suicide is a final, para-doxical attempt to boost their own self-esteem.

The 'broken home' interpretation focuses on another aspect of the phenomenon. It stresses the dire effects of losing one or both parents through death or divorce. The statistics show beyond all doubt that children from broken homes are at more than average risk of committing suicide. However, family therapists have also observed seemingly complete families in which unconscious death wishes are directed at one individual. If the person concerned kills himself, then, according to the theory, he is simply carrying out a death sentence, imposed – albeit tacitly – by the rest of the family.

There has also been debate about the influence of upbringing on the development of suicidal tendencies, especially the amount of punishment and affection expe-rienced by those who end up taking their own lives. Many psychologists believe that readiness to commit suicide is a learned behaviour. In other words, patients show a tendency to want to kill themselves when life gets diffi-cult because they have experienced seemingly hopeless situations a large number of times in the past. The term used for this pattern of behaviour is 'learned helpless-ness'.

In addition to these and other psycho-social theories,

there are physiological factors to consider. Whilst there is no such thing as 'a suicide gene', a genetical determination can probably show itself in the way emotions are controlled, thus making it easier for the person to act impulsively. In a major personal crisis this could be the factor that determines whether or not someone ends his life, or hesitates and then decides to go on living after all.

Taken together, these medical-cum-psychological interpretations all reflect the notion of an 'unsound' streak in some human beings. They describe various factors that can increase the risk of a suicidal reaction to a crisis. But something that causes one person to commit suicide may cause another to sidestep the problem and yet another to respond in a bold or perhaps even creative way.

Interestingly, sociologists and doctors pay little attention to the motives identified by would-be suicides themselves. Researchers usually assume that suicidal behaviour is the result of autonomous processes of which the person concerned remains wholly unaware. Many doctors therefore regard suicide as a pathological symptom; and the notion of an illness that leads to suicide (known as 'a pre-suicidal syndrome') has found its way into medical textbooks. The chief characteristics of this syndrome – first put forward by the Viennese psychiatrist Erwin Ringel – are perceptual constriction, death fantasies and inhibited aggression, which ends up being turned against the self. Ringel's departure point here is Sigmund Freud's psychoanalytical definition of suicide as an attempt to resolve an aggression conflict.

The idea that suicide is an illness is a controversial one. However, there can be no denying that many suicide letters display both a constricted view of the world and a turning of aggression against the self. This is exemplified in the suicide letter of a seventeen-year-old schoolboy: 'I yearn for an end, an end to this torture. A sweet end. I'm longing for it, I hate life, I hate everything, I'm totally lost, I'm a human wreck, am I just imagining it – I don't know, I'm completely at its mercy, I'm lost for my whole life, I don't know why, I just have such a strange feeling.'

High-flown passages of this kind often depict suicide as inescapable. In the words of a man who felt inexorably driven to action by the situation he found himself in: 'That's the law of nature, and I'm submitting to it'; or in the words of another man: 'It's as though everything were in the hands of fate.' Some suicide researchers view such observations as symptoms of a psychopathological process. Their critics, on the other hand, wonder whether it is always appropriate to define the peculiar emotional state of suicidal individuals as 'pathological', and whether suicide cannot perhaps be regarded as an understandable human reaction when it occurs at a moment of total personal breakdown or after a succession of painful failures or losses.

Suicide as a Means of Solving Problems

The woman mentioned earlier who killed herself in the flat of an uncle, a practising doctor, asked if her uncle could explain her actions to her husband 'in medical terms'. This touch of irony hinted at her freedom of choice as an individual. Even at moments of complete failure and breakdown, human beings are free to choose whether or not to resist the impulse to commit suicide. For this reason it will probably never be possible to predict with any certainty whether or not someone will take his or her own life.

There is a third approach to the problem of suicide – that those who kill themselves are not simply the victims but also the agents of their own destiny. This approach explains suicide not by what drives people to take their own lives, but by what they set out to achieve, what prob lems they seek to resolve, and what means they choose to use.

The French sociologist Jean Baechler has identified a whole spectrum of possibilities: escape from an intolerable situation; self-punishment; revenge; emotional blackmail; cry for help; self-sacrifice; or letting fate decide the outcome. In most cases there is a mixture of different reasons. The African student quoted earlier declared in his suicide note that he had decided to kill himself because a denunciation by a fellow student had made him an object of universal contempt: 'It was decided that I should return home. But I prefer to kill myself.' This sounds like a resigned acceptance of death as a means of escape. At the same time, however, he also twice mentioned the name of the person who had denounced him, and so was clearly hoping for revenge, even though there is no explicit mention of it.

Many writers therefore make a distinct effort to combine their suicide with a 'good deed'. After killing her three children, and just before taking her own life, a woman writes to her husband: 'I've done this so that you'll finally come to your senses, do you understand what I'm saying?' Her entire letter is written in the manner of a schoolteacher scolding a pupil. But did the woman really believe that the letter would be a salutary shock, or was she trying – in the interval between murdering her children and killing herself – to contrive a morally acceptable explanation for her monstrous acts?

Suicidals Make their Protest

It is in the nature of things that those who talk about suicide are mostly not those who do it. It has to be said, however, that there are no clear boundaries when it comes to self-destruction. Erwin Ringel, one of the pioneers of suicide research, argued that there is a whole continuum of suicidal behaviour, ranging from suicidal thoughts through self-harm and attempted suicide to suicide itself. After the Second World War there arose an international movement dedicated to the prevention of suicide, and based on the optimistic premise that potential suicide victims could be identified in advance and given appropriate treatment. So-called Suicide Prevention Centers were set up in more than a hundred towns and cities in the USA.

Since the mid-1970s, people who have been affected

by medical suicide-prevention measures have made a massive contribution to public debate on the issue. The writer and commentator Jean Améry, the philosopher Wilhelm Kamlah and the author Hermann Burger all published books setting out their personal take on the pre-suicide phase in great detail; all took their own lives soon afterwards.

Writing as people not far from ending their lives, they articulated their own particular viewpoints. In his *Meditatio mortis*, for instance, Wilhelm Kamlah lamented the fact that 'those who seek to kill themselves – and actually manage to do so – not only take upon themselves the stigma ordained by traditional morality, but are also forced to serve as a repellent spectacle to a shocked world.' Hermann Burger, a severe depressive, sought in his *Tractatus logico-suicidalis* (published in 1988) to create 'one last crumb of understanding'. He tried to convey the almost unimaginable difficulty of carrying on living, insisting that a 'depressive deserves public acclaim for each day that he manages not to kill himself.' Jean Améry – who had declared in a 1976 interview that the idea of killing himself had been familiar to him 'pretty much since childhood' – also tried to put into words what the prelude to suicide felt like. Améry identified utter defeat and failure as the central experience of those who kill themselves, using the French word *échec* for the sake of even greater intensity of expression.

These defenders of suicide were accused of glorifying it. Améry retorted that he wasn't interested in founding a 'Suicide Club', but was speaking solely for himself.

What Kamlah, Améry and Burger wanted above all else was to be allowed to end their own lives in a dignified manner. All three were accordingly damning in their indictment of contemporary medicine, whose lifesaving interventions they condemned as formalistic and degrading. For Hermann Burger there was only one possible antidote to suicide, and that was love; but therapy, he said, does not produce love.

The psychiatric camp countered by confronting the protesting suicidals with the results of suicide research. These showed that suicidal patients were only rarely absolutely determined to end their lives; in most cases they were ambivalent about it. Their sense of total failure was purely subjective, so the argument went, and they were quite incapable of being objective. Furthermore, their ability to make rational decisions was pathologically affected by the pre-suicidal process.

The problem with this debate – which is still going on today – is perhaps that it is too heavily focused on finding explanations that can apply across the board. The question 'To be or not to be?' remains, after all, a purely personal one, no matter what constraints society may put in place.

Does Suicide Fit in with Today's World?

'It is a plain fact that heroism has become an inappropriate means of resolving conflicts within the community of mankind, be they major or minor [. . .] Just as heroism – one man's solitary decision to settle a conflict at a stroke

– is growing ever more obsolete (however seductive it may remain for the individual), so too suicide, the most solitary of all decisions, will come to seem inappropriate – anachronistic, one might almost say.' This prophecy was delivered in 1988 by Professor Hans-Ludwig Wedler, the then president of the German Society for Suicide Prevention, and statistics over the last twenty years appear to support his statement. Certainly suicide rates in the UK have decreased over recent decades and in 2003 were at their lowest since 1973.

What could account for this? Should it be put down to the sustained effect of preventive measures? Or is it explained by the increase in drug-taking and therefore to a protracted form of self-annihilation that does not go down in the records as suicide? Or have people become more flexible, so that the desperate are resorting to alternative courses of action? (A psychiatrist told me that one of his patients resolved his suicidal crisis by simply buying a last-minute air ticket and flying off somewhere.) Or has less and less care been taken over examining the corpses? There is some evidence to support a number of these possibilities – but no proof. The phenomenon remains a puzzle to suicide researchers. All that is certain is that suicide has become less common over the last twenty years as a means of dealing with inner conflicts.

Suicides nonetheless remain shocking and disturbing events, even though they are now treated in a more matter-of-fact and professional way. Increasingly there are dispassionate TV and radio contributions on the topic, books written by relatives of people who have died, and discussion forums on the Internet – where one can also find the suicide notes of the Nirvana singer Kurt Cobain and others, or advice on where to find help when in a suicidal frame of mind. Even the trend for webcam exhibitionism has reached this previously taboo area. In July 2001, for instance, a twenty-nine-year-old New York teacher took sleeping pills in front of her webcam and then collapsed. An Internet surfer saw this happen and called the police, who saved the woman's life.

Has suicide lost its appeal, now that its mysteries have been explored and shamelessly exploited by an entertainment-obsessed society? 'Every good suicide requires an even better suicide note, without which no one of sophisticated taste these days would dream of slitting his throat.' This barbed witticism appeared in summer 2003 in the satirical Internet magazine *ZYN!*, which then casually provided some tips on how to write a truly professional suicide note: 'Get it all off your chest, don't mince your words – but don't forget to apologise for being such a wimp that you can't even write a proper suicide letter'. Mockery, irony or malice: the disparaging laughter of others can fill someone who is in the depths of despair with rage. But to be enraged is to be alive.

Letters

1

Dear W,

9.00

I know that nobody will understand me. A year ago, I wouldn't have understood it myself.

But today I feel that I just can't take a single step further, that <u>nothing</u> is fun any more. That's why I'm doing it. I just can't go on any more.

I haven't even been happy about you, about my children etc. My life has lost all its substance. I tried to fight it, but it just seemed as if there were all sorts of obstacles that I couldn't overcome.

See you,

9.30

I think I just let things get on top of me, but I didn't want to admit it. So I felt dissatisfied.

9.45

*I feel totally indifferent to everything – for weeks now,
I've often cried about it when I've been alone – nobody
can ever understand what torture it is.*

13.10

I've achieved my aim.

After beginning his suicide note to his wife, F set off in his car
at around 10 a.m. on 17 June 1983. He drove south down
the motorway. He was supposed to be on official business at
that time, so he wasn't missed by his colleagues. About 125
miles away from where he lived, he drove his car onto a path.
There, he poured a gallon of petrol from the reserve can all
over himself, before setting himself on fire.

Eyewitnesses who happened to be passing saw smoke rising,
and found a man lying on the ground, unclothed and seriously injured. The grass was burning all around him. They should
leave him where he was, he told the people who put out the
fire; he wanted to end it all.

F, a twenty-eight-year-old fire service employee, was considered by his colleagues to be a quiet, reserved, exemplary
character with a reasonably happy family life. He had only
recently begun to suffer from his nerves and had been
complaining of headaches. The tablets prescribed by the

doctor hadn't worked. Very depressed as a result, F had been treated by a neurologist. Papers found in his car by police investigators called to the scene, showed that he had arranged a further appointment with a psychiatrist.

While searching the car, the police found the hand-written suicide note on the passenger seat. Its final sentence – in which F says that he has achieved his aim – makes it sound as if he'd already found salvation – but this hope remained unfulfilled. For F, death was a prolonged and agonising business. Doctors later established that F had firstly slashed his wrists; he had then tried to hang himself, before taking the petrol canister out of the boot as a last resort. Although 75 per cent of his skin had been burnt away, it was nine days before he died in hospital.

2

It has to be,

yet I can't do it. – It has to be!! I'm afraid. It isn't easy to overcome fear, but I have to do it. Fear is weakness!! If only I knew why, when everything's going to be so easy and lovely. Sleep, eternal sleep. Death. – Oh, how that word sounds. It has to be lovely. It has to be, it has to be. Farewell, farewell!! Take care!

B

But I don't have any choice. I love R, but it's too late.

3 o'clock. Just a few minutes until the gas releases me. I'm smoking one last cigarette. The gas is making a noise, it's hissing fear into me. Really. Even though I know that everything will be over then, I'm still afraid. I'm sorry, I'm feeble . . . It has to be. Farewell, go your own way! Farewell!! Your beloved brother, to whom you were every-thing. Don't tell Mum . . . accident

B

So I'm a coward after all. I'd never have thought it. The gas just keeps on hissing! It's terrifying. I feel as sick as anything. A roaring in my ears. I've felt the fear of death, but I know that I've got to overcome it. My skull is buzzing, I still can't hear anything. I'm really scared now. Or at least I imagine I am. And yet it has to be. If I had another cigarette, I'd smoke. I'm going back under the covers. I feel heavy now. Quite strange. It's as though everything were in the hands of fate. If I'd had the courage to take my hand off the tap, I'd have done it ages ago. Now it's happening again. If it weren't for the hissing and the fear, it wouldn't be half as bad. But it's not fear. Caution? In case I die? Honestly, now I feel like laughing. I want to die, but I'm afraid of it. My heart aches. Now I'm going again. For the last time. Now I'll lie still. Bye! Bye!

B

5 o'clock. Have to puke. I'm afraid, cowardly dog that I am. Afraid of release. Perhaps I should have stayed sober. Is it the alcohol that's getting to me, or the gas? Either way, I feel sick. Sick as a dog. What now? I have to die, but I'm too . . . cautious. But no. I'm quite hot. It'll soon be over. Bye, H, I'm afraid, coward that I am. Not like me. Now I'm going. Now. Now. Now. Never thought dying would be so difficult. But I have to do it all the same. Adieu. Adieu.

B

I'm not a coward, but dying so young . . .

I'm a cowardly dog. Zero prospects, and then this fear. Now I'm going for a pee, and then –

I can't do anything about it: I have to, have to, have to, have to die now. Slowly, slowly, slowly. I hope I'll see it through this time.

Third attempt. My head. The roaring.

Do you know what it's like to put the covers over your head and turn the tap on? Not a nice feeling. I'm still afraid. But now I'm going. Smiling, because he's waiting for me with a smile.

The gas is disgusting. Foul. But now I'll pull myself together. Hard, hard, but I have to do it. I think it's diffi-cult, and yet it's easy.

Never to see the sun again. I'll smoke one more . . . Should I live again? No! No! No! Dead. Gone for ever. Take care. My cigarette is finished. Now here we go. I'm afraid. Farewell!! For ever. Farewell!!

B

These notes by a twenty-three-year-old man, B, were found with a long suicide letter, and were quoted in a 1973 essay by Dresden suicide researchers Helmut Kulawik and Dieter Decke. The detailed description of his last hours seemed significant to the two psychiatrists because it showed so dramatically the ambivalence surrounding both the decision to commit suicide and the actual act of suicide. The notes seemed to confirm a thesis by the researchers' colleague and former boss, Professor Karl Seidel, that writing a suicide note is in itself a vital part of the process of deciding to kill oneself. According to Professor Seidel, writing a suicide note finally puts an end to the ambivalence felt previously about whether to commit suicide or to carry on living. The twenty-three-year-old man died of gas inhalation after writing his last 'Farewell!'

3

Dear W,

These are my last lines to you. Now you won't have to provide for us any more. Ordering the coal is all your job, it's up to you to sort it out. Now you can also pay off the fuel bills for this house, fuel bills for a whole year in the other house, the whole year's rent for the other house. With your Christmas bonus and your salary, you can pay everything off and start a new life.

I have such a small allowance for food for ten days, three children and myself. Tell me how I'm supposed to manage. I never went out or treated myself – everything was for the children.

No need to go and sort out S's nursery place, I've already told them he's leaving. You won't find it difficult to start from scratch again. We've had a good marriage ever since I – well, ever since the beginning of December. It was just as I imagined it would be. I could cope with our huge debts then. By New Year, I'd been so looking forward to having sex for the first time, and I knew it would give me an orgasm. But you just taking me in a *drunken state was disgusting. I got nothing out of the sex, and I've hated it ever since.*

I made up my mind that we'd leave you for ever. It was quite painless, all three of them were fast asleep. I gave them all tablets and beer beforehand. None of them noticed anything. It all happened very quickly. Now that I know they are all dead, I can do it too. I gave them life, so they will die with me too. Believe me, it's better for them this way. It took a lot of doing to end their lives, it was very hard. But that won't bother you. Now you don't have to carry on living in an empty marriage until they're grown up and are able to understand that they've got to get along without a father. But just watch it: don't force your future wife to have sex if she doesn't want to; and be a decent father, as you have been ever since December. Don't get into debt again, and only spend as much as you can afford.

For example: you buy three crates of beer, but the fuel bills and rent haven't been paid. Duty must come first, and you can enjoy and share out the little bit that's left. Do you get my drift?

Pay off all the debts first, then have a family, start a new life. All we can do is learn from our mistakes; you'll soon forget the children and me. Of course my mistake was cracking up, but there's no going back for me: what's happened has happened, and there's no going back.

On that one day I wasn't in hospital, because I was already five months gone and they refused me a termination. I spent the whole day at the station, reading. There has never been another man in my life. You were the first and last person I had sex with. I've never had anyone else. I have loved you and hated you.

You are an excellent father and husband, I grant you that. You help your wife around the house, and you know how to bring children up. I have loved you for that. But I've hated you for not being able to control your sexual feelings even a little bit.

Above all, you have to learn that in future you first pay your rent, fuel bills and newspaper bill, then calculate how much of your salary is left over for you to live on, and how much of the remainder you can afford to spend on other things.

Well, I'll end here, as it's time. This is how I want it, I can't go on, it's over for ever. Believe me, it's for the best. You're a strong character and you'll soon forget us and start a new life. May you have great success in your future life, and much happiness in love.

Warm regards from all of us,

Your children H, S and I, and your wife K

PS There's some money in the bag with roses on it. I

should have blown the lot, because you never gave a thought for the children either when you bought motor-bikes, a car or expensive binoculars – only about your own pleasure. My sole vice was baking, and that was it. Get rid of the three crates of beer, and you can pay these two bills from our holiday.

I've done this so that you'll finally come to your senses, do you understand what I'm saying? I'd never have managed without a job and all the rest of it. I'd still have been dependent on you because I don't have anyone else. But I can't do it any more, even though we had such lovely times together and even though you gave our children a good life. But that doesn't count nowadays. First you have to do your bit and do your duty. Only then can you afford to buy something for yourself.

I can't see any other way to make you open your eyes. On my own, I'm too weak and too dependent on you. I'd always be the underdog. If I'd had at least one person to help me and to look after the children every now and then, I'd have fought to the end. But as it is I don't have any alternative. The children and I have had a couple of nice days together – I had to do this because every argument with you inevitably has a bad effect on the children, and this way I can prevent it. There's a letter for the police in the desk, top left.

K

KP killed her three children before killing herself. The letter to the police was worded as follows:

So, these are the last lines I shall ever write. I gave three children their lives, and have taken them away again. I made sure no one noticed anything. I did my three children first – then the next day, once I was sure that none of them was alive any more, myself. I'm weak, and wouldn't be able to start a new life all on my own I don't have any qualifications, just debts, and no proper career.

I've never wanted to have a fourth child. I was refused a termination in the fifth month. I've got no strength of character. I have nobody who could support me if I were to start again. That is why I have done it. I think it's for the best, for the children too.

With kind regards,

K

Dear Schnucki!

Please forgive me for what I've done, but I love you so much that I can't be without you any more. I hope you have a happy life; once I'm out of your way, you might be a bit more sensible and keep your hands off married men. Lay red carnations on my grave just once.

Nothing is known about the background to Mr P's suicide or whether his accusations are justified – but, by contrast, much is known about its *effect*. Although P's letter appears at first glance to be reconciliatory and romanticising, it and the actual suicide itself made the woman named 'Schnucki' feel unbearably guilty. The following day she wrote to her parents: 'I can't get over the fact that everyone will say I drove Herr P to kill himself. But believe me, I'm completely innocent; I never cheated on him'. She killed herself the same day.

Dear J,

By the time you have this letter in your hands I will be
in the process of causing my parents and (~~my and~~)
perhaps you great distress. I have done many wrong
things in my life, but I promise you all, all of you whom
I love and cherish, and that includes you, that it's the
last distress I'll ever cause you. Or didn't you know how
much I loved you, you must have noticed, but you're just
not capable of love any more. I'd never have believed that
I could demean myself the way I've done with you,
though I knew right from the start that you were just
playing with me.

And when I now depart this life – something that
disgusts me – please don't think I'm not thinking about
my dear sweet child, but I don't have the strength to start
all over again. Knowing you as I do, I doubt whether
you'll spend any time worrying about it, and I want to
ask you not to do so, because I've already been bitterly
disappointed once before. You knew it, but you had no
pity for me, you just dealt me yet another blow. And if

I'm going now – I already feel sick – I love you just as much as I did on the first day.

Your R

Sorry about the handwriting, but I'm in the kind of state where neat writing doesn't matter any more.

The suicide note of R, a nineteen-year-old woman, was published in a medical dissertation, along with some background details. According to her mother and a female friend, R had an eight-month-old illegitimate child by a married man. She had become pregnant again by her current boyfriend, and had tried to induce an abortion herself, using soap solution. When she became ill with peritonitis, she was too frightened to go to hospital. Meanwhile, her boyfriend had abandoned her.

The young woman used the pesticide E605 to take her own life. This poison had become notorious a few years earlier as a 'dead certain' suicide method after massive press coverage of the trial of a woman in West Germany who had used it to commit multiple murder.

6

My darling G,

As you destroyed the first letter, I'm writing again. This is definitely the last you'll ever hear of me. Yesterday evening (Sunday), you said that you were divorcing me come what may. Regardless of what happened. I'm not angry that you – so you told me – had already had, or were still having, a relationship with another man. Though it was a huge blow to me. Not least because you always used to tell me that there hadn't ever been anyone else. I just don't understand how you can faithfully promise me 'I'll never leave you, whatever happens'. And now this. You don't even give me the tiniest chance. Even if my visit to the doctor on Thursday had had a positive outcome.

You did say that your nerves can't, or couldn't, take any more. But don't you think it was the same for me? And in order not to destroy you (because I love you), I'm putting an end to it. If you still can, then forgive me for what happened in the car this morning (Monday). I don't know why I did it. I'd probably blown a fuse.

I've already threatened you with suicide several times, but you probably never believed that I'd do it. As you can see, I've now made it a reality.

Maybe if you'd been a bit more affectionate and tender (at any rate recently), it would never have come to this. I don't know. I know only that it's something I absolutely longed for.

But now see for yourself what you've done. In my first letter, I think I wrote that you shouldn't blame yourself, and that my decision came entirely from within me. But now I'm sorry to say that you share responsibility for my death. Even on Sunday evening (13.3.), you didn't even try to stop me. Your reaxion was just 'Go for a bit of a walk and calm down'. It wasn't fear of dying that stopped me shooting myself, no, but the thought that shooting myself might get you into strife with the police. I don't want this whole thing to cause you any trouble. You don't deserve that.

I increased my insurance with Mrs B today. I know you're not that bothered about material things – but in that case put the money by, if only for the children's sake. If I can't do anything else for them now, then I can at least help them financially when they're older. I've told you everything now. Bear in mind that the car speedo belongs to H-J. The other (new) one is on the shelf in the garage. The key for the hay-bunker is there too (tied to a door handle).

Please believe that I never wanted to put pressure on you with my suicidal inclinations. You should always be free to decide what you should do and what you have to do. Now you've decided to leave me. But I just can't cope with it.

Shape your life, and our children's lives, in such a way that you're happy and fulfil all your desires. Perhaps your new man will be able to give you everything that I'm afraid I couldn't give you. I'd have given all I possessed if I'd been lucky enough to make you happy just once. It wasn't to be.

But as you told me yourself, that's what the other man can do.

I have this certain feeling that I'm ending my life as a failure and a dead loss. I'm sure I've only got myself to thank for that because of my childhood (gas). But you know all that. If I'd known then how things would turn out later, I reckon I wouldn't have done it. Because you, the children, and your family have shown me for the first time how lovely a family can actually be. Unfortunately this time has now ended. I deeply regret that. But you leave me with no choice.

I don't want to be alone. I was alone until I met you. I know what it's like not to be able to share your problems with anyone.

If you can, then forget the bad times with me. Perhaps there were a few nice hours as well that you can think back on.

All I can do is tell you once again that I love you and have always loved you.

Be happy

H

On 17 March H, a policeman, went for a doctor's appointment. His problem: erectile dysfunction. Two days previously, his wife had announced that she was seeking a divorce. Nevertheless, she accompanied her husband to the doctor. During the consultation, H told the doctor that he had been fantasising during the journey about 'crashing into a tree at top speed and killing myself and my wife'. But he hadn't done it, he said, because it wouldn't solve anything.

His wife told the doctor that she had found a suicide note from her husband a couple of days previously. She had tackled him about this, and he had promised not to commit suicide. A day later, though, he had got up during the night and had pointed his gun at her. However, said his wife, she had managed to talk him out of killing her and then himself.

At this point in the conversation, the doctor asked them to bear in mind that he was obliged to report these things to H's superiors at work. Both H and his wife asked him not to do so. After consulting his colleagues, the doctor decided not to report anything in order not to provide grounds for a renewed suicide attempt.

Towards the end of the conversation, H asserted that he had in the meantime started to feel more hopeful again and that he would make plans for the future. The doctor discharged him with instructions to find a psychiatrist in his hometown and then to come back and see him again on 24 March. He impressed on H's wife that in the meantime she wasn't to give him any excuse to start making suicide plans again.

Three days later, on 20 March, H decided to move in with his parents. His wife had confessed that she had already been secretly seeing one of his colleagues for the last six months, and now planned to marry him.

On the evening of 20 March, this colleague came to see H because H wanted to speak to him once more before moving out. When he appeared, H was initially struck dumb; he'd thought of countless questions on the telephone, he said, but now he couldn't remember them. During the course of the evening, though, the pair did actually talk about the imminent divorce, about sexual problems, about how the house was to be divided up, and about future contact with the children. H gave his wife's lover to understand that his world had collapsed. The first time his wife had announced the divorce, he said, he had tried to hang himself in the garden. But now, he said, he had got over that.

While H's wife prepared the evening meal, the two men agreed not to regard one another as enemies. They said they would see each other again on 22 March, and then the divorce papers could be submitted to the courts.

Fearing a violent act, H's wife had already hidden her husband's gun in her safe a week previously, and had given the key to a neighbour. She was aware of her husband's suicidal tendencies; he had turned the gas tap on once before as a schoolboy. When and how the policeman had managed to retrieve his weapon remained a mystery to the investigators. He had presumably secretly stolen the key, taken the gun out of the safe, and then taken the key back to the neighbour's house.

On 20 March H slept for one last time in the marital home. The next day he shot his wife and then himself.

H's wife's lover, who was questioned by the police the same day, recalled a remark which he hadn't thought particularly significant during his visit the previous day. H had apparently said at some point during the conversation: 'I'm not going to hurt anybody'.

– My dear Mum, my only dear Mum,

I'm sorry, but it's my same old pain again!

– Leave me in peace, I've been searching for it for ages.

– Life is hell, just meaningless, nobody understood me.

– I couldn't go on living.

– At last I'm experiencing death, life was terrible.

– Life is just pain and bad luck, it hurts.

– I didn't want to be disappointed yet again.

– What's happened this evening is all just coincidence!

I only love G, right to my very last breath.

– F was my first man, he has to believe this.

– Please tell G that <u>I loved him</u>, it's <u>revenge for F.</u>

– <u>Forgive me, G.</u>

*– I'm afraid I'm having to take a promising young pilot
with me.*

*– Forgive me for taking a promising young pilot with me,
dying's easier when there are two of you.*

– I tried to <u>forget</u> everything, even today.

– <u>F is blameless!</u>

– F and me, my victim.

*– Please tell G I really loved him, he <u>never</u> understood
me!*

– I can't feel the gas any more, sorry. . .

*Goodbye, G! I loved you! My darling G! Please forgive
me! The man lying next to me is just an unfortunate
coincidence, both of us gassed, want to pray to God. Save
my child! Bury me next to Daddy! Life is dreadful, please
forgive me.*

When twenty-two-year-old K's father broke into her flat he discovered two bodies. He had never seen the naked man on the
sofa before. (The police later ascertained that he was an air force
pilot.) K was lying on the floor next to the cooker, dressed
in her underwear. She had laid her head on a newspaper,

on which she continued scribbling farewell words to her mother until she lost consciousness.

Another part of the newspaper lay on the table, on which K had written a second suicide note to her fiancé G.

The post mortem was held on the same day, and showed both deaths to be the result of carbon monoxide poisoning. K had turned the gas tap on, fully aware that she would take the man sleeping on the sofa to the grave with her. She had known the pilot for years, but only in passing. On the previous evening he had accompanied her home from a dance.

K was seriously depressed, as the police were able to discover from a letter written by her fiancé. She had married two years previously, had had a son, and was divorced a few months before her death. Before the divorce was finalised she began a new relationship, but something did not seem right with this relationship either. As she wrote to her fiancé, she felt as if she were on the edge of an abyss. He wrote back that she was a mystery to him.

Before turning on the gas tap, K sealed up the door that led to her two-year-old son's bedroom with a rolled-up blanket. The police found a newspaper by the flat door with four words scribbled on it in pen: 'Please save my child!'

8

Dear A, dear G,

*Many thanks again for taking such good care of me
when I came to visit. It was a lovely day. Believe me, I
could only enjoy it because I knew that it would soon
all be over. Otherwise it would be unbearable. . .. I
can't be happy without the knowledge that the end will
come soon, and I never know when I'll be overcome by
crying. . . The reason I was so relaxed with you was a
dream I had on Monday night. E was waiting for me
somewhere on a ledge of some cliffs by the sea. I
couldn't see E himself. He was just like a grey shadow.
The very fact that I knew he was waiting for me made
me happy. But it wasn't at all easy to know how I was
supposed to get down onto this narrow ledge. There
was a danger of plunging into the sea. By thinking
ahead and concentrating really hard, I did then
manage to do it without falling in. From there, we
could move carefully onwards to our right, to get to a
place where there were other shadowy figures. And this
made us feel happy and free. . . You just can't imagine
how relieved I feel now. I'm just going on ahead of*

you. At some time in the future, you'll go too. . . So, now it's time, take care.

The writer of this letter was a housewife in her late fifties. Her husband, E, had died five months previously.

9

S,

I can't bear the thought of life without you. You mean more to me than you can ever imagine. The path I'm taking now is definitely the wrong one, but I don't know of any other way. I hope you'll remember me kindly despite all the mistakes I've made. I love you, and the thought of this makes the step I'm taking a little bit easier, because I can't fight for your love – that's an option you never allowed me.

I wish you better luck than you ever had with me.

Take care,

R

You were all that I had, but what do you want with a failure and a wimp like me. I'm not angry with you, so please don't be angry with me either.

Neighbours had noticed the smell of gas and had called the fire brigade. They had to break into thirty-one-year-old R's flat. The dead man was lying in the kitchen in front of the cooker; three of the four gas taps were open. Before his death, R had switched off the doorbell and had disconnected the fridge. On the coat rack in the hall lay a sealed envelope addressed to S.

She was a waitress and, according to her colleagues, R had only met her two or three months prior to his death.

Sunday 28th December

My dear, good R!

I must thank you for your Christmas letter and gifts, and for the love and kindness you've shown towards me yet again – I just took your letter and set off on my travels with it on the morning of 24 December; it was terrible, I can't bring myself to think about how I spent Christmas Eve and the whole Christmas holiday period wandering around the streets, alone and deserted and shut out of everything – it was all more than I could cope with, and I ended up in the worst possible spirits. – Why am I telling you this? R, I can't go on any more. I'm not railing against my fate, it's all my own fault – but I have to find peace somehow, and that's why I'm asking you to forgive me as I've forgiven all my adversaries; please make peace with me, and let me live on in your heart as I did in our happiest days. You will be my last thought this evening, and with this thought I'll go to sleep as

Your loving N

10

The writer of this letter was being prosecuted for embezzlement.

11

Dearest Uncle,

Forgive me for doing this stupid thing in your flat of all places, but I was sure that I'd be able to take the step from life into death here undisturbed. I can't go on living now that M has chosen the other one. I beg you to make sure that this other woman doesn't bring up my children, I'd rather they went to a children's home.

Tell M how much I loved him; perhaps you can explain my actions to him in medical terms. I know he doesn't deserve me doing such stupid things on his account – but I love him, and I can't go on living without him.

I've got one more sentimental thing to ask of you: play a Beethoven sonata once you have read this letter, the Moonlight perhaps, and think for a moment how much I liked hearing you play.

A last kiss on your cheek from

Your G

By the time you receive this letter, you'll already have heard from someone else that I'm no longer alive.

Now you've got what you wanted and you have my husband all to yourself – if he still wants you.

I just hope you've got enough of a conscience to see that you are to blame for what I'm doing.

I hope your marriage to my husband produces at least five children!

G

G, the twenty-five-year-old mother of two children, had recently returned to studying. She was found in the kitchen of her uncle, a doctor; she was sitting in an armchair covered up to her hips in a quilt. Gas was streaming from two wide-open gas taps. The letter to her uncle was lying on the kitchen table. The other letter was sent in the post and was addressed to her husband's new lover.

According to her husband, her suicide had been preceded by five weeks of huge rows because he had begun a relationship with another woman. When his wife and his new lover happened to encounter one another at the couple's weekend retreat, a major confrontation ensued. G's nerves were in such a state that she could no longer follow her lectures. Her uncle wrote her a sick note. Five days later, the couple had another major row. Before leaving her husband at home on his own, G secretly pocketed the key to her uncle's flat.

12

17th May

H

I couldn't be the kind of husband you imagined having. I have used a rope to put an unnatural end to my own life so that you will be happy. Don't cry. There's no point any more. What's done is done.

Even you didn't know how to make a man of me,
Despite all your aims, there were too many

My last wishes

1. <u>No</u> *funeral*

2. <u>No</u> *grave*

I want to be scattered to the winds!

I want to be forgotten!

K

_H_

I had to do it because you didn't care about me and were just waiting to do something foolish. I did it for you, so that you can find a better life. Men have always fancied you and you'll soon forget your husband except for your son.

I wanted to have some nice years, too. We <u>missed out on a lot</u> because of my job

<u>My last wishes</u>

1. No funeral

2. " grave

3. Ashes scattered

4. Forgotten

S, a policeman, hanged himself in the attic of his house on 17 May. Before doing so, he wrote these two letters – it's not known in what order. He put the dated letter on the living room table; he put the other letter into his breast pocket where it was found by the police.

S's death represented the conclusion of a marriage full of conflict and contradiction. According to police investigations, the discord began after his wife had an abdominal operation that left her unable to have any more children (she already had one son). In the period following the operation, she told the police, her husband had sometimes pushed her away and called her a 'harbinger of death'. They were divorced, but S, who had wanted a divorce, still continued to visit his ex-wife on a regular basis. A year later, the couple remarried.

The rows began again when the wife found a love letter addressed to her husband by another woman. On the other hand, a rumour went around their small town that S's wife had been spotted going off in cars with other men. What actually happened was never discovered. The only thing known for sure is that S became extremely possessive about his wife, who was evidently attractive. He started making regular visits to the pub, where he got drunk. At home he verbally abused his wife, sometimes hitting her as well. Their son secretly kept a record of his father's violent behaviour.

In January, when S beat his son as well, his wife called the local police – i.e. her husband's colleagues. This was highly embarrassing for him, and also led to disciplinary measures being taken against him. S subsequently toyed with the idea of resigning from his job as a policeman. Finally, on 17 May, he suddenly got up from the family lunch table for no apparent reason and declared that he wouldn't be needing anything more that day. Up in the bedroom he ripped up whole heaps of paper and stuffed them in a sack. He sat with his family for one last time to drink coffee. Afterwards, his wife busied herself with the washing, and he retreated to the attic. There he downed a bottle of wine and then hanged himself from

the stairs. He must have dashed off the suicide notes immediately before (hence the numerous mistakes and the one
letter that breaks off in mid-sentence).

13

Dear T,

Right up to the very last you get no consideration from me – I'm terribly sorry – please forgive me. I've lost my grip.

Even your guiding principle – that the will just needs to be there – made me feel even more desperate.

I've always admired you and held you in high regard. You're a unique person, and you've always helped me. But now you couldn't help me any more. I know you're strong enough to go your own way without me.

I was always a misfit in this world.

I've been a real burden to you, especially over these last six months, because I've known for six months what I was going to do.

I owe you an explanation, too.

Someone called Dr L had me completely under his sway.

I was like a piece of paper that he could crumple up and flatten out, and then crumple up again. I've tried to find some stability with you, but I just couldn't manage it any more.

Please don't go looking for Dr L, and don't let him come looking for you. He's completely inhuman. You're human. I don't want him to be there on that dreadful day either.

Please forgive me. I couldn't think of any alternative.

U

Please: no white shirt.

My black dress and camel coat.

UT was a thirty-seven-year-old engineer with a large chemicals company. One day in June her husband arrived home from his shift to find his wife in their bed, wearing a red and black summer dress. She had laid her head on a white towel. Her poisoned body was already cold.

Mr T could offer the police no explanation as to why his wife had taken her own life.

Both he and his wife had wanted children, but their fourteen-year marriage had remained childless. According to the husband, it had recently looked as if she might be pregnant after having suffered two miscarriages; U had consulted a doctor with regard to this. Generally, he said, there had never been any serious differences between them. His wife had just seemed depressed; she had cried without telling him why.

Mr T suspected that another man might be involved, but cast these thoughts aside. Not until her death did the situation become clear. U left a package alongside the suicide note to her husband. The note that accompanied it read: 'His Hamilton syringe is in the packet along with a book and a present he gave me that I never liked. Please inform Dr L.'

On the day following the suicide, work colleagues told Mr T that his wife had been having an affair with Dr L. When questioned by the police, Dr L – married with two children – confirmed that this relationship had been going on for two years. Moreover, while searching the flat, police found notes made by UT, who had kept a diary of their clandestine meetings. They had repeatedly clashed because of Dr L's refusal to upset his existing family. UT had shared intimate details with her lover, so he knew that her problems with pregnancy were due to her having been sexually abused by her father. He also knew that the very painful medical treatment she had undergone hadn't produced clear results, and that following it the doctors weren't prepared to guarantee that she would be able to have a child. This, he said, had made UT terribly depressed. Dr L also claimed that his lover had a problematic relationship with her husband. As a result, he said, her husband had often gone off to their allotment alone at the weekend, which was when he, Dr L, was able to visit her in her flat.

After one such visit, UT told her husband that their shared home was completely dead and that it lacked 'an artwork of some kind'. That, at any rate, was what Dr L had said.

14

Farewell letter – no more joy

No more joy, no more love,

No more sun or moon to see,

A little bit nasty: just a corpse.

Not very nice for you either, I reckon.

The sun gives warmth, love, strength.

The moon is cold and white

Clouds deprive the sun of its strength,

But the night is clear and bright.

I've often dreamt of beautiful things,

All I've found is smiles.

If ever I rebelled

I gained nothing – just pain and anguish.

It sounds resigned; that's what I am.

Life has stolen my life away.

It can all be so simple, but I went off course

built up stupid hopes

Such a pity about my love.

Love was strong and beautiful.

But time is stronger.

It makes you forget.

May I be forgiven for my fit of sentimentality.

I wouldn't have made a very good poet.

These lines, written by a sixteen-year-old schoolboy, were printed in a medical dissertation. Suicide notes by adolescents typically combine high-flown, poetic phrases with philosophical speculation on the meaning and/or pointlessness of life.

15

Dear E,

Today is the last day I'll ever sit next to you – you probably won't understand why I ran away, but believe me, I had no other option. Because you were and are my best friend, I'll give you the most valuable thing I own. In my schoolbag there's my folder with my Gojko pictures and my diary. There's just one thing I want you to do: take care of my Gojko pictures. They were always my favourites. Don't try to find me, because I'm never coming back. I'm going to tell you my biggest secret: I'm in love with a boy who won't look twice at me. Now I think that I might have written down my own life in my book Vera. But I hope that everything will turn out ok. I don't think any of you will find me alive. Believe me, E, you were my best friend. I entrusted all my secrets to you, even my biggest secret of all.

My novel will never be finished now. I'll give you this novel as well.

Please forgive me for taking this step. Forgive me if I've

*ever done you any harm. But I don't want to waste any
more time now.*

For the very last time, regards from your friend,

Λ

*Don't look for me, because I don't know myself where I'm
going.*

The boy I'm in love with is called KN.

*It's possible that I'll kill myself with ordinary painkillers.
But I don't know yet what I'll actually choose. But then
of course you'll see it for yourself and find out for
yourself.*

'The most valuable thing that mankind possesses is life': this
sentence from Nikolai Ostrovsky's *How the steel was tempered*
was read by thousands of children in German schools. Fourteen-
year-old A, however, valued her collection of photos of the
actor Gojko Mitic (who starred in German films about American
Indians) and her unfinished novel much more highly.

She took an overdose of tablets but there is no information
as to whether or not she survived her suicide attempt. The
wording of her suicide note was passed on to the local
education authority.

16

May peace, health, Heaven's mercy,

steadfastness and strength be with you all, my dear family. With this, the last letter that my hand has written to comfort you and give you heart, I have taken leave of you for ever. I have made my decision and have hurried away to rejoin my beloved sister. I do understand that I will cause you unimaginable grief and suffering. But I didn't have the strength to go on living any more; my hopes have been destroyed; I've decided to take this ultimate step. In order not to be saddened by this, take comfort from this little letter written in my own hand.

An Ethiopian named B passed on a letter to the foreigners that I had sent to our embassy and in which I listed various problems which arose not from any weakness involving my studies but from my life within the community here. After that they treated me with utter contempt and excluded me from my courses. It was determined that I should return home. But I prefer to kill myself.

My dear father

Your elder son, who was bold and decisive and never bowed his head, has been taken from you, and taken from you because his hopes came to nothing. I know that I have caused you unimaginable suffering. But these people have taken me to the point – and I don't know how they've done it – that I hate my life. Be strong, don't be afraid, take comfort, my dear father, farewell for ever. May my mother, my grandparents, be strong like my father, and find comfort.

My dear brother

I clearly remember the last time we saw one another at Bole Airport. Alone among my relatives you stayed to the very end; your eyes twinkled as you kissed me farewell. That was our last day. Now you're the only son who can give our father and mother strength and comfort. Now you're responsible for the family and you're the one who will carry on the family tree. Now that my hopes of seeing my dear brother have vanished, I'm sobbing as I say goodbye to you – farewell for ever.

My little sisters

Although I've often thought of you and have wondered how I can help you, these have remained unfulfilled hopes. I left you suddenly and unexpectedly because my

hopes of studying and returning home were dashed by
Ethiopians seeking their own personal gain.

Support one another, comfort my parents and yourselves.
Keep a good eye on my only brother. Sympathise with my
father and comfort him; and ease your own sorrow by
crying. Make sure you follow this, your brother's last
piece of advice. I think people die elsewhere as they die
in Ethiopia, there's also death elsewhere, and as you've
not died yet, we'll meet again in the future. Thus I have
made this firm and bold decision, and I've gone on ahead
of you. Farewell for ever.

<u>My beloved relatives</u>

Support one another. Above all, don't forget my father
and my only brother. Comfort <u>my father</u>. My hopes of
seeing you again have been dashed. This door is closed
to me now. I'd give anything to open it again. Now I'm
hurrying, crying, to my brother and sister who went
ahead of me. I know and am sure that I've given you
comfort, eternal comfort. But heaven and earth have
become too confined for me. Although mother earth is
so big, there's no space for me any more. Just leave it,
she told me. The people thought bad things about me
and wanted to destroy me. The one who did it to me
was an Ethiopian named B. Now I've left you because
my plans to return to my own country, to work, to eat
and to help you, have been destroyed. Farewell for ever.
With this letter, written by my own hand, I'm taking

my leave of you. Comfort one another and be strong.
Farewell.

<u>*Mr P; Mr T.*</u>

I ask you to look after my father and my family. I hand
over all the work in and around the house to you. Help
them! Help them! Look after them, regard them as part
of your own work. Now I bid you farewell, too, farewell
for ever, I'm leaving you.

Mr P, I ask you in particular to support my father, my
mother and my only brother.

For those of you who will never find me again, I remain
your brave and resolute brother whom you'll never see
again.

L

This Ethiopian student was visiting other foreign students,
whom he scarcely knew. Soon after his arrival, and to the
horror of his hosts, he threw himself to his death from the
seventh floor of the hall of residence.

17

Something is turning me

into an animal; I have to obey it and act accordingly. Something is dehumanising me, making me lethargic, forgetful, depriving me of courage, without telling me its name. I feel despicable, I'm lost, it's just the way I feel, I don't know why. I yearn for an end, an end to this torture. A sweet end. I'm longing for it, I hate life, I hate everything, I'm totally lost, I'm a human wreck, am I just imagining it – I don't know, I'm completely at its mercy, I'm lost for my whole life, I don't know why, I just have such a strange feeling.

Give everyone who knows me my fond regards, my kind regards, everyone, everyone who knows me, and help everyone who comes to you, who asks you.

VS, a human being

An exaggerated and objectively speaking unjustified high opinion of oneself, an inner void and neurotic searching for the meaning of life, the loss of inner equilibrium due to the collapse of any real relationships with other people

*and endless doubt, vacillation, and torment, a lack of a
sense of duty, so that practically anything is permissible,
lacking any great goals or real inner incentives and any
good, honest sense of determination.*

[. . .]

*I would like to confess that over the last few weeks I've
got myself into a state which I can't get out of.*

*A mad feeling, consisting of countless undigested
impressions and experiences from every conceivable
sphere of life which I encounter.*

*A perfectly normal process, actually, but I never got to
the stage of analysing or discussing it with other people,
because I've spent the last few years neurotically – as I
see it – destroying all the real relationships I had with
other people. My belief that this is neurotic is what gives
me the courage to say that I haven't been acting irrespon-
sibly.*

*I ask you not to view my death too tragically because the
moment that's coming is one I've been longing for for
ages.*

These are extracts from a letter written by VS, a sixth former who had just turned seventeen. The sixth former also wrote a second letter, in which he made accusations against various people, gave details about the poison he used to commit suicide, and gave instructions about what was to be done with his chess board, guitar and tortoise. Neither letter had a specific addressee.

... when you're not in control

of your feelings any more, when you lose all sense of
time, when things seem to swim around you, when you
barely notice if someone is talking to you, when you
haven't got the strength to answer either, when everything
you do just disappears into a cloud of cotton wool, when
you just mechanically carry out your daily duties . . .
when, when, when . . . I don't understand myself any
more, I don't understand the others, they don't understand me – why am I actually here – on this planet –
why not on another? Why was I born here, why don't I
live in another part of the world, why these incomprehensible coincidences? Why am I one of the preferred
ones who live whilst others die of starvation or never
experience the advantages of a so-called civilisation? Or
do I live several lives? Did I have a previous life? How
can I know whether everything that's handed down to me
is right? Nobody can help someone else to order his
thoughts or take away his fear of dreams which prophesy
disaster rather than fulfilment, which he can't shake off,
even when you act in front of other people as if you were
happy, when you try to surrender yourself to the moment.

Can it be <u>her</u>? Or is <u>she</u> deceiving me and the others as well? If only I could talk to <u>her</u>, but she might laugh at me, tell the others what's going on in my head. All the same, I sometimes think she should at least hear me out. Just for once – just for once, I'd like to see what it's like to open your soul to someone else . . . I'm going to do it, but preferably on my own, alone – nobody must blame themselves, nobody must cry, who is ever really to blame for someone else blaming themselves, who's to blame for anything at all? No, tears don't help . . .

This letter was written by a sixteen-year-old sixth former KM, who died after taking an overdose of tablets. The letter, which had no addressee, left his parents completely baffled. They couldn't imagine whom their son could have meant by 'she'. They had known nothing about any relationship with a girl. The only thing they had noticed was 'an ever more evident sense of melancholy'. K had, they said, become increasingly withdrawn, and they had no longer been able to get through to him.

19

Goodbye letter

I'm sick of life so I've killed myself. This shitty family just takes advantage of you. I was always being blamed for being what I am, okay I agree that some of it was true but not all of it I can't cope with it any more so I think the best thing for me is to die. And what's more I was never corled by my proper name but was just called filthy swine, dirty swine, bloody swine, lazy swine and it's too much for me and I've had it please don't burn me but funeral me or bury me or whatever it is in the Northern Cemetery next to [. . .].

I'm leaving you now/Sunday 30 November at 4.15pm

This fifteen-year-old hanged himself in his bedroom. After their son's death his parents told the police that they constantly had to reprimand their son because of his slovenliness, and to this end they called him a 'filthy pig' and a 'slob' and told him his room was a 'pig-sty'. Neighbours also claimed to have heard the mother calling her son a 'swine'.

Leaving aside whether the insults were justified or not, there is no doubt that this boy was the family outsider.

At school he was regarded as bright and amusing, and was well liked by his fellow pupils. According to an assessment by his teacher he was very keen to do well, but had to put in a lot of effort to get good results. His character had apparently shown itself particularly clearly during sports lessons. He had reacted very impulsively when anything went wrong, and couldn't bear to lose.

As an enthusiastic sportsman, he was keen to get into a specialist sports school. An accident shortly before the entrance examination scuppered his chances, whilst his older brother (whom his parents held in higher regard) did manage to get in. When he got into fights with his brother, he mostly lost, whereupon his brother called him a 'drip' or a 'washout'. Just minutes before he hanged himself, he went away from his brother telling him: 'The next time you come it'll be me that wins'.

20

27th March

Property of R and H

for our parents . . .

When you see the dates, you're bound to be horrified and think that we've had it in mind to do this for ages. Yes, it's true, it's just that many of our plans were wrecked and had to be re-made. For this has to be a guaranteed ticket to death.

I, H, started writing this notebook quite early on. This notebook doesn't contain just my views, but R's too. He didn't write them down because he's not very good at spelling. It's not particularly well ordered, I've thrown out some boring pages, crossed some things out and written other things besides.

We want to emphasise here on the first page: it's not your fault!

Dear parents,

We have decided to die because there's nowhere on earth that you can enjoy the peace we both long for, and because we're firmly convinced that there will never be total peace on this earth. For it starts with people torturing and killing animals for no reason, and then do it to their fellow humans too. War rules the world for ever! And we ask ourselves why, oh why, do people keep inventing ever more dangerous weapons if they're not planning to use them somewhere?

We can't escape this world – so full of problems, loneliness, chaos, luxury, and strivings for power and infinite wealth – in any way other than the one we've chosen: for our duty was to find ourselves and then to grope our way forward regardless of where it led: our souls have no home. We started our search full of hope, but hope dwindled as time went by. A little spark that turned to desperation, endless desperation, deep and painful, with just one hope for peace: in death!

'For here have we no continuing city, but we seek one to come' (Hebrews, 13, 14).

As realisation dawned upon us, we found many obstacles in our way. But we've never tried to do anything other than live out whatever was coming from within us!

We believe that our earth is becoming just a concrete

bunker. It is increasingly losing its connection with immanent nature, and has an empty, sad visage. True, we have to some degree got used to finding the world unpleasant, and started to live inside our own selves, and were able on occasion to forget everything outside. But humans are sensitive beings, and neither of us managed, unlike many others, to accept life's lot. Please believe us when we say that we've tried and tried to give effect to our own take on life as much as we could. But we're shut in a cage; a cage that may be made of gold, but one that deceives people. Barely do you think you've taken a step forward when you bump up against a brick wall: commands and prohibitions everywhere!

We're not made for this competitive society. We don't belong to the mass, the giant flock of sheep, that all wander around together like plastic people. 'Just don't stand out, stay nice and safe within the mass!' – that's <u>their</u> motto. But it's <u>not ours</u>!

We asked ourselves a thousand times what the meaning of life was, but society, too, just gave us evasive answers or no answers at all. Yet we asked ourselves: what's so good about spending your whole life as a bank clerk or being a secretary or wearing yourself out as a manager?

Humans are bound from birth: birth dooms us to die; genetic inheritance makes us a product of nature; sociali- sation makes us the product of our environment. We are just little wheels in the massive social machine, so small that you could miss us. And that's why we'd have liked to have asked all humans (or many of them): 'Okay, so don't you see that your lives aren't fulfilled, but that at best just a few moments of them are?'

We two, we have this honourable way out. Okay, it's hard, harder than just deadening your feelings. But on the other hand it only takes a short time, not a whole lifetime.

You needn't say that we didn't face up to problems, because that's not true. You know what? We felt as if we were on an escalator that was travelling the wrong way, and no matter how hard we tried to get to the top, we just couldn't manage it.

And believe us, downers like these lead to depression and utter despair. And every day was a downer for us, yes, every day! For the role play would begin first thing every morning: at work, with our parents and other people. The only time we got to relax was in the relatively short time we were together. This role playing is very tiring, and you quickly get exhausted by it. We didn't like our jobs. They weren't over- or under-demanding, but we felt useless.

We aren't going through puberty, and I'm not pregnant. This isn't some naïve act, but the result of a year's deliberation. We don't want people to pity us, nor do we want them to shake their heads over us. Seen from the outside, we really did have everything that anyone needs: good parents, good brothers and sisters, and plenty to eat and drink.

But death is the only way of feeling a breath of freedom: whether you're 10 or 100, no one can stop you choosing this path!

In our opinion, death isn't something terrible, but something kind. Bearing in mind all the evil things that go on in the world, death is man's best friend! It's like cool water after a life as hot as sand. Our hearts will be silent and no longer complain, and our feet will become tired and will no longer long for the dust of endless paths!

'As for man, his days are like grass; As a flower of the field, so he flourishes. For the wind passes over it, and it is gone, And its place remembers it no more. But the mercy of the Lord is from everlasting to everlasting On those who fear Him' (Psalms 103, 15-17).

Maybe everything is now clearer to all four of you; maybe you're totally confused. We do know that we have caused you great misery by doing this. But you've no reason to be sad! Rejoice with us, for we are happy to have found this path to self-destruction!

'But I would not have you to be ignorant, brethren, concerning them which are asleep, that ye sorrow not, even as others which have no hope. For if we believe that

Jesus died and rose again, even so them also which sleep in Jesus will God bring with him' (1 Thessalonians 4, 13-14)

We hope that beyond the grave, at least, there are no barriers between Catholic and Protestant, because our wish is to be <u>cremated and buried together</u>.

Our funeral should be very plain, with the smallest possible number of mourners. Our coffins (assuming one's needed for cremations) should be as simple as possible. Moreover, we'd prefer not to have any gravestone, but one simple wooden cross for both of us. We want no flowers on our grave, let alone wreaths. We don't want any death announcements either. It's to be a cheap funeral without any big display, because we hated all that stuff when we were alive! The money saved could be better spent on a donation to 'Bread for the World'!

Our funeral should not be sad, because you have to remember that this is and remains our <u>own</u> decision, and that means that we wanted it to be exactly like <u>this</u> and <u>no different</u>.

'In the world ye (we) shall have tribulation: but be of good cheer; I (we) have overcome the world' (John 16, 33)

Our brothers can have everything of ours that they want,

and we hope that you will give our pets good and loving homes.

Don't cry for us, because we're taking a permanent holiday from life, and we're happy about it!

Please don't be sad!

For we, R and H, are humans, and as such we have lived in all those that came before us – and shall go in living in all those that come after us! We shall live on in people's dreams, in their sorrows and fears, in their goodness and their badness, in justice and injustice, in the strong and the weak.

As erstwhile true human beings – who have been planning their own deaths for nearly six months now – we shall live for ever in the rest of humanity, so you mustn't be sad about what we're aiming to do.

This is written by us, R and H, who have been eternally lonely and lost.

This document by two German teenagers was published, with the parents' permission, by someone who worked for the Samaritans. He added that this letter wasn't just devastating, but was also a 'signal, a cry which we older people have to take deadly seriously. For what is so lucidly expressed here matches the feelings of many of today's teenagers. They want to quit a society and civilisation that offers them no scope for feelings and desires of their own, no space for closeness and warmth, no time for dreams, and no convincing models for a fulfilling and meaningful life'. He wanted to make people think by publishing it, and wanted to provoke his – the parents' – generation into talking about 'our hidden wishes and dreams – our unresolved feelings – our burning longings, for instance for love – our half-asked questions'.

Nothing is known about the lives of either of the seventeen-year-olds, or about their family circumstances or possible areas of conflict.

H took her own life on the night of 20 September. Nobody knows what happened to R.

21

To Class 10b.

I hope this letter I'm writing now will tell you a bit more about me. You know just as well as I do that my life hasn't been the best. I always got on well with you, even if there was trouble every now and then.

I'm on the brink of carrying out my decision to put an end to my life that isn't actually a life at all. But there's one more thing that I'd like, and that's for you to play the Beatles song 'Eleanor Rigby' for me. This song, about a priest, talks about my problems too.

I'd better finish now.

M

An adopted child, M found himself in an inhospitable house-hold. His adoptive father was often drunk. According to the report sent by his headmaster to the local education authority,

M also found learning things very difficult. For the information of the education authority, an extract from the lyrics of 'Eleanor Rigby' was included with the report.

Dear parents,

I have to write this to you or I'll find no rest. I'm sorry to have to do this to you, but I don't have any choice. I can't cope with my life. Nobody tries to understand me, and you can't either. Dear parents . . . It's not right for you to know that I hate you, but I don't want to cause you any more worries. I'm sorry.

No further information was available about this note.

15 November

Dear parents, dear sister K, dear relatives. Today I want to write my last ever lines to you. I'm going to do something that I won't be able to regret. You all know how unstable I am. I can't stand it here on board. You really do get driven to jump off. It's <u>almost</u> entirely my own fault, that's why I'm going to make yet another mistake, and one that can't ever be rectified. I've always done everything wrong and I've never got the hang of anything very much. And I regret that I ever went to sea. I should have listened to you three months ago, but I'm afraid it's too late now. I'm going to jump overboard with my life jacket on; it's 99:1 that I won't make it.

If I should happen to be fished out alive by a steamer, I'll be in touch again. But as I say, 99:1 it won't happen. If I look at all the trouble I've already caused, anyone would think I was mad, and I think that myself too. I'd like to thank you for the understanding you've always showed to me. I always wanted to be free, but never realised that home is still the best place in the entire world. You've tried to understand me, you've given me a good home, but I couldn't accept any of that. Then I kept trying to make everything right again, but I just kept freaking out. By the time you get this letter, I may already be dead, unless I'm in luck and manage to survive. Drop a line to M and put some money into C's savings account. These are my last two wishes. Please carry them out for me. Best wishes from your son R.

R was a sixteen-year-old seaman. When he wrote his last letter he had already been at sea for an unbroken period of just under two months. About sixty-five men, including many Spaniards and Portuguese, were on board the fishing vessel. It was the second voyage for R. The first time, he had worked in the galley; this time he was a deckhand. The ship was initially victualled for 100 days, but then took on additional provisions and fuel from other ships. That meant that the boat would be at sea for more than three months, and that the crew wouldn't be home in time for Christmas. In a general atmosphere in which human contact was lacking and the pressure was on the men to perform, R could only manage to talk about his feelings openly in his letters to his parents. Ten days before his death, he wrote: 'I've been away from home for almost four months, and I'm homesick at least once a week. I'd never have thought that three months could be so long.'

R. was seen for the last time on 15 November at around 9.30 p.m. At half past midnight, his absence was noticed as he was supposed to be on watch. The captain initially thought that the young crewman was hiding somewhere, and had the ship searched. During the search, someone noticed that a life jacket was missing. Only then did the ship turn round and retrace its course. Three more ships became involved in the search operation. Visibility was good initially; later on, light snow began to fall. The water temperature was four degrees centigrade.

Dear all

3 lots of deadly nightshade, ill for 3 days, dizzy, weak,
confused, big eyes, work was very difficult on Monday
because you can't let anyone notice these things, until
you're dead, you can't let anyone notice 30 primidone 20
valiums, used up a whole month's spending money,
nausea, weak, obviously affecting my brain, confusion,
decreased alertness etc. Work very difficult on Mon . . .
it's interesting to see what happens afterwards, but death
will be a whole lot better.

It's coming up to the second anniversary of 3 January. I
think I've got the right amount together. You've all got
used to me not being there and so almost not existing.
We do everything for a reason. I want to become 100 per
cent an object, instead of always being neither this nor
that, just something in between. I've talked it all through
with the objects here and they tell me it's not before
time. I've got the entry fee (poison). I've caused enough
unhappiness. The big mistake was 2 January 1984 (it
was carelessness, but it almost seemed as if I'd committed
murder) Which certainly wasn't the case. Of course that

was just one among the many disasters I caused you. In order to avoid causing even more disasters when I return, I'm just not going to return. It's not worth my living in the social sphere either. I don't fit into the narrow frame of human society. I'm just too different. The conflicts are too great for me to somehow pursue my interests. It was clear to me that I could only pursue my interests in secret and only to a limited extent. I deprived myself of this last possibility by my stupidity on 2 January. Though my constant thieving could have had the same result. (no longer possible) What's more, suspect I'm not bright enough. With that I'll say goodbye.

LT had been in prison since March 1984 when he killed himself. His fellow prisoners viewed him as strange. On the one hand his cellmates were impressed by his knowledge, and he helped them with their crosswords; on the other hand they thought he was mad and teased him. LT increasingly retreated into a bizarre world: he bred moths and watched them develop. He read scholarly books, dissolved copper in acid, or lit small fires. He had been under special observation since the middle of 1985 due to his peculiar predilections.

One of LT's more striking characteristics was that he would go to the toilet and tip into it cakes or infant milk formula that he'd bought specially for the purpose. He told his fellow inmates that things felt hunger too. He sometimes talked to the wash-basin as well, and said he could hear the voice of his sister, who had taken her own life at the beginning of 1984.

New Year 1984 had been the turning point in his life. In the months immediately before that, he had carried out a string of burglaries. Showing exceptional skill, he had managed to break into two schools, a chemist's shop, a grocery shop, a dog club, a DIY shop, two farms, a dyeworks, a private house and even a barracks without leaving any traces that could be spotted by the police. His aim in all these break-ins was simply to get bits and pieces that he needed for his chemical experiments. He had built a 'bunker' on his parents' land for this purpose.

For New Year's Eve 1983, he made his own fireworks which flew 500 feet and which experts classified as explosives. At the same time, there were problems at home because his father disliked his sister's boyfriend and wanted to force her to leave him. During the night of 2 January the sister killed herself with prussic acid, which her brother had stolen from a school shortly beforehand. The search for the source of the prussic acid led the police to the brother, whose illicit store of chemicals was duly seized. He was sentenced to eight years' imprisonment for breaking the law on poisons and explosives as well as for theft.

Immediately after the second anniversary of his sister's death, LT mixed himself a lethal injection; his suicide note hints at guilt feelings. The twenty-two-year-old had got hold of the syringe in prison and had kept it hidden for months in a tube of skin cream. He had been to see the doctor, claiming to have insomnia, and was given sedatives which he secretly hoarded until he had a sufficiently toxic quantity.

Even though fellow inmates told him that the voices he could hear above the empty loo and fall pipe just came from other prisoners, right to the very end LT clung to the idea that objects had 'a soul, a consciousness, and a certain intelligence'. He noted: 'They know exactly how much information to give at any one time, and they know what they can and can't tell if they want to stay out of trouble'. He underlined one sentence in his extensive notes on this 'phenomenon': 'objects learn something every second, and never forget a thing'.

25

They used the most foul tricks

to try to wrest my job from me. My failure – caused because I had such a vast amount to do – wasn't the only reason for it. My life over the last couple of years would in many respects be the stuff of novels. If the man concerned should happen to be able to interest the relevant people, I would ask him not entirely to forget the part I played (a very passive part admittedly), and for instance to give a donation to the Jewish Old People's Home in the event of financial success. My private wishes have been extinguished by a combination of bad eyesight and the inhibitions inflicted on me by my upbringing. I had no influence on the beginning of my life, but I am going to have an influence on its end.

This suicide note was written by C, a fifty-three-year-old auditor, thought to be suffering from some form of schizophrenia. C had apparently made frequent calls to the police alleging 'damage to property within her dwelling caused by persons unknown'. Each time, she would unlock the heavily bolted door and complain about non-existent damage and devastation.

26

Before I take my leave

of this world I'd like to give a personal account of my life. Though it's really just one part of it of special significance in my life – the last eight years.

When I was a child my father brought me up to think it was very bad to have ideas of my own. Then once I'd left home I couldn't relate to the world around me. My existence centred only on me and my own life. I couldn't cope with problems and instead passed them on to other people. My life began to explode after my stag night. I married a woman in order to give her life some meaning. Now I know that I didn't have the right to do so.

Conditions were imposed on me by the country that debased our marriage and turned it into a mere tool of the country's instruments of power. After that, all I could think about was punishing anyone and everyone who passed judgement in the name of the people without even the slightest moral right to do so. But I chose the line of least resistance.

On 21 April I murdered G, the sailor, and then S. I'd told him about it, and he was going to report me. He's been in my cellar since November. This week I stabbed J and A. I don't know why. But I think that the violence inflicted on my life by the day has given rise to a matching counter-violence.

To be honest, I wanted to use my gun to kill others as well: police officer M, F, and my former colleague B. I'm letting them live in the hope that they will die a long and painful death.

C

After he had shot himself in the head with a home-made gun, C, a thirty-three-year-old man, was found seriously injured in his flat. His criminal record included numerous convictions for offences including deception, grievous bodily harm, theft, and driving under the influence of alcohol.

The police found the suicide note in his house. On investigation, his confessions turned out to be largely accurate. A body was found in the cellar of his house. He was also strongly suspected of killing the two women, J and her daughter, A. The only doubts about his confession related to the murder of the sailor. Detectives considered this particular confession to be false because the man's step-brother had already been 'convicted of the crime and condemned to life imprisonment'.

It is thought that the reference to 'violence inflicted on my life by the day' could have been a mistake, the product of a crazed mind, and in fact he meant to write 'by the state'.

27

Tape transcript

Dear R,

I find it very difficult to talk about the questions that are bothering me at the moment. Our marriage has collapsed. We lived together for nineteen good years; things were harmonious; there were never any big problems. We grabbed hold of life together. And suddenly it's all over and in the past. I would like to thank you for the lovely years we spent together. Our marriage produced [two] children whom we greatly enjoyed. Everything was lovely, but it will come to a sad end all the same.

A man appeared in your life, K, who couldn't cope with his own marriage, who had problems, who beguiled you, whom you couldn't resist, who wrecked not only his own marriage but in effect mine or ours too.

I did have this feeling that there had to be a man

*involved in our marriage over the last weeks. We talked
about it several times. But you were too cowardly to
admit it. What I saw on Friday made me even more
certain that someone else had intruded on our marriage.
The discussions we had afterwards proved to me that you
no longer love me, that you now only love this man who
you don't really know very well, who you just happened
to work with, and who you said you're not having
intimate relations with. And yet this is your big love, and
all at first sight. I hope you're not disappointed.*

*This has swept away nineteen years of my life; I'm
surrounded by shattered fragments. I have always loved
you, and still love you now, I'd be able to forgive you, but
the conversations we had showed me that so far as you're
concerned, it's no longer possible to work our way
through this together.*

*This is why I have decided to get out of your way. I can't
say yet how it's going to happen. By the time you listen
to this cassette, you'll know. I've arranged to meet K at 2
p.m. I don't know how I'll react; my nerves are shot to
pieces really, and I can't imagine carrying on living
without you, starting all over again and building a new
life for myself. I'm thirty-nine, almost, and at the moment
I don't have the will to live any longer. If I can find the
strength, K will go the same way as me; if not, oh well,
I'll go whatever. I have somehow summoned the strength
to do it and have taken all the necessary practical steps.*

I want to thank you again for the many happy years we spent together and wish you all the best. Carry on bringing our children up to be decent people, and carry on enjoying your life and job, and forgive me for all the extra worries and problems I'm causing you now.

I have a few practical requests. I would ask you to make sure that my official stamp, my army identity card and the two telephones are taken back to my place of work, that you please pay a bit more into the communal account, and that you give the files to G. Please give Fanny Hill back to A. I did actually want to read it, but I won't get round to it now, for life goes on, remember that. The car is supposed to be checked on Tuesday. If you don't take it in, do at least give them a ring, or you'll lose your slot and you won't have anywhere to take the car.

I expect the bill for the gravel will be arriving shortly. We don't need the gravel any more. Talk to J and A about selling the garden or leasing it – after all, you're not interested in it. It should bring you 40 to 50 thousand. That's all I wanted to mention.

I wish you much joy and fun. Please forgive me my behaviour, but at the present time, in this situation, there's nothing else I can do, I'm sorry, take care, all the best, bye.

[short pause]

A postscript after listening to the tape. I forgot to mention my life insurance; I'm sure you won't get the pay-out in the circumstances. Cancel the contract, please, but you're sure to get the money I paid in.

I think that's all. I've got nothing more to say, but want to tell you one more time that I loved you, that I still love you now, and it's a shame that our marriage had to take this course. We'd certainly have been happy together for the next twenty years. I'd planned to do so much with you, but sadly it's no longer possible.

I'm sorry, so very sorry, that I won't see how my children turn out, how they grow up and become decent people, or so I hope.

That's about everything. I've got nothing more to say. Take care, and once again: I wish you all the best and hope you and your life turn out well. Bye.

Early on the morning of 10 August an employee at an industrial site discovered two bodies and a car that didn't belong to the company. One of the dead men was Lieutenant K, a security officer. The other was a thirty-eight-year-old professional soldier identified by investigators as Senior Ensign B.

The investigators quickly ascertained that B had decided 'while in the grip of a mental disturbance showing pathological features to kill his purported rival K and then himself'.

B's wife was K's secretary. K's marriage had been in trouble for six months, and the closer his divorce came, the greater were his secretary's hopes for the future.

On 7 August, B confronted his wife, saying that he had seen her exchanging intimacies with K. She responded by telling her husband that she was very attracted to her boss and wanted a divorce. B reacted aggressively; he told her that she would come to hate him. Then he grabbed the telephone and arranged to discuss things with K on 9 August. B used the intervening day to steal a gun from work. On the afternoon of 9 August, the two adversaries drove to an industrial site.

K's body was found in the passenger seat; he had been shot in the neck and temple. B's body lay fifty feet away on the ground, his right hand still clutching the gun. His head bore a single bullet wound: he had shot himself in the forehead at point-blank range.

28

Dear Mr S,

Today is the day of reckoning for what you done to me and my wife. I've suffered a lot during this year since the divorce. Can't bear to look at the swinish things you done to me any more. 14 years I worked and she got the lot, the whole lot. I didn't even get a bed. That's the thanks I got for 14 years' work. She's getting her thanks back today. My car's to be sold, and the money's to be put into my kids' savings accounts in equal shares. Please don't dump my kids the way you dumped your own.

So you've got my whole household now just see how you cope with that. Your wife will be delighted but she won't take you back. The year since the divorce has driven me crazy. I don't know what I'm doing any more. But I'm not going to end up in prison because of you that'd be too big a price to pay for that slag. It's been an awful time for me. I've not been able to sleep at night for months. I don't have any choice. Yes, you're going to be punished for your swinish behaviour now. I pulled my 4 kids out of the gutter and the thanks I get

*for that is paying child support without even being
allowed to see my own children. It didn't have to be
like this. I was good for 14 years and now all of a
sudden I'm just shit. You've got my whole household
now just see how you cope with it. If you dump my
kids nothing at all belongs to you it's all the children's.
I loved my kids that's why they're to get the money for
the car. Whoever's intrested in my tools can have them,
I haven't got nothing else. My parents have got the log-
book. I'd have died of misery anyway it was all her
fault.*

*During the divorce I gave her my whole end of year
bonus and the thanks I got was having to pay for the
court and the lawyer. It was a terrible time. She even
wanted the car as well, tax, insurance, child support,
rent a garage, even though I built it with my own hands.
That really pissed me off. I'm ashamed because of my
children but I don't have any choice. If her mother was
still alive it wouldn't have come to this. If she hadn't cast
me in such a swinish light maybe it wouldn't of come to
this it's done my head in I don't know if I'm still quite
normal, that's what it's all done to me. Now you've got
your punishment for what you did to your wife and your
3 kids.*

*I gave her 1 year to come back to me that time has
already passed but now it's over. I'm not too cowardly
to throw myself under a train but I'm not going to
prison. She's not worth it. If you dump my kids the*

*shoot's yours including the bedroom suite what's at LK's
and my car. But please don't dump my kids. Cos all
this whoring about, it's not their fault. They don't
deserve it any different Your wife will be pleased and
I'm punishing my slag something terrible. I made a
nice nest for my kids I can't do nothing else for them
now. If she'd had given me just the bare essentials I
might have got over it but not even so much as my
duvet. Now here's my grissly thanks for what you
swines done to me.*

W's marriage was dissolved in May; in June, his former wife's
new lover (Mr S) moved in with her. W, who refused to accept
the divorce, repeatedly visited his wife and gave her a series
of ultimatums. He demanded that she hand over various house-
hold goods, argued with her about financial matters that
hadn't yet been settled, and demanded that she should get
back together with him within the year. He threatened her
new lover with physical violence; S, however, ignored it, which
made W even angrier.

On 3 May W went to his former wife's house, knowing that
she arrived home at around midday. The four children were at
school. They presumably argued in the kitchen, and then W
killed his wife with a hammer blow to the back of the head.
He then wrote the suicide note to his rival, left it in the kitchen,
and locked the kitchen door. In the living room, he consulted
the train timetable to see when the next train was expected.

Taking the kitchen door key with him, he fled to the railway and threw himself under a train that was passing through right on schedule at 1.01 p.m.

29

I've wanted to talk to you

but I didn't dare because I was afraid of what your answer would be.

Without you, nothing here has any meaning for me any more. I love you like I've never loved anyone before.

But it isn't your fault: it's my mistake that things have come to this, why did I ever start it. I'm choosing a very easy way out for myself, and I'm getting out of your way.

I'm leaving with thoughts of you.

My watch and wallet are in your work jacket.

Twenty-eight-year-old R had already served half of a two-year prison sentence for theft. As he was considered quiet and level-headed, he was in line to become head prisoner in a communal cell. His suicide came as a total surprise. It was only when they read his suicide note that the prison authorities discovered that he had fallen in love with another prisoner. The object of his unrequited love had distributed the food on the day of R's death. 'I don't need food any more,' R had told him. He then went into a storeroom and hanged himself.

30

Dear Mr K,

Don't be shocked, when you read this I won't be alive any more. I've made a calm decision – however paradoxical that may appear – and I hope I'm doing the right thing. It's infinite weakness that is responsible for this sacrifice, but not resignation. Don't mix up the body, which I couldn't simply dissolve into nothingness, with me the person. I'd like to ask you to be so kind as to put a doctor in the picture before you do anything else. Cause of death: prussic acid. I hope you'll accept that, and not drag me through all that police and anatomy business! All the best to you and your wife,

HB

PS Please take charge of the key for the time being – it's in the corridor (near to me, on the small table)

Do use my telephone. You don't need to worry about the poison in the air – it's spread out throughout the whole room, so it's not too concentrated. But open the window straight away, and be careful when you remove the plastic bag.

My dear loved ones,

This isn't pessimism or carelessness. I've not got the strength to carry on. I've tried to get help, but I can't go on using psychological crutches. Please forgive me if I'm imposing an even greater burden on you by leaving. That's the law of nature, and I'm submitting to it. I've completed my circle, even if I never perfected it. Stick to life and to the truth. It's thanks to you that I didn't do this any earlier.

H

21 May

You couldn't help me.

On the morning of 21 May, HB's neighbour found the first suicide note, addressed to him, outside the door of his flat. He didn't enter his neighbour's flat, but called the police. When the police entered the flat they noticed a faint smell of bitter almonds. The second suicide note lay on the desk, addressed to his relatives. HB himself was dead. He had pulled a plastic bag over the top half of his body and then inhaled prussic acid.

HB had started seeing a psychiatrist a decade earlier, after starting to feel persecuted or watched. According to expert opinion, he displayed 'schizoid symptoms', such as shyness, unsociability, an inability to mix with people, a lack of warmth and kindness, along with eccentric tendencies – but no manifest illness.

His mother remembered her son once saying that he wouldn't wish a life as hard as his on anyone else. According to her, H had had a perfectly normal childhood. He was nine when he and his parents left Pomerania as refugees. H completed school and university with flying colours. He worked hard in his job as a research engineer, often working until late at night (though this was also partly because he had difficulty sleeping). His marriage collapsed after three years. His mother went on record as saying that she didn't know whether he was involved with a woman at the time of his death.

Two days after his death, HB's telephone rang, and a woman asked for him. She told the police that she had been on intimate terms with him over the past year. He had, she said, told her that she was his ideal woman, and had put a lot of pressure on her to get a divorce, sometimes calling her 'at the most ridiculous hours' just to hear her voice. She said that HB was a 'strange and complicated' person, who spent his whole time philosophising about the meaning of life. He was 'a bit loopy'; when she had wavered about the divorce, he had told her that he had some poison that would work in seconds. Following that, they had discussed suicide several times. HB had wondered how he could arrange things so that his family – of whom he was very fond – wouldn't remember him as someone who had killed himself. In this context he had talked about possibly engineering a car accident.

On the evening before his suicide, HB had visited his lover one last time. He was desperate to stop her going to her husband the following day. She, however, stuck to her decision.

She rang him again from the station. He was in total despair, she said, and gave her ten minutes to get there, otherwise it would be 'the end'. 'I took it to mean that our relationship would be at an end,' she told the police. 'And I was pretty glad to hear it, because the whole thing had become such a strain.'

31

Dear E,

My health has collapsed; my business has collapsed:
there's just no possible way I can carry on living any
more. That leaves you facing a lot of things. But you've
turned into a strong man. You're so capable and self-
confident that you'll be able to master anything.

Be good to Mother and your brothers and sisters. Even
though Mother and I are divorced, I still think well of
her. May she think the same of me.

You take charge of the employee insurance papers, and
get an expert to sort out the pension. Mr L might be able
to advise you.

Don't get drawn into taking on the liabilities of my
company. That's an inheritance that you have to turn
down.

Be nice to Mrs K. She's been a friend, and she's
worked with me fantastically unselfishly to the point of
self-sacrifice.

I commend W [the dog] to the care of Uncle A who, incidentally, has done everything possible to save my business; but I just can't manage it physically any more.

Mother will be able to support C and D on her pension until they can stand on their own two feet.

Dear E, if there's any way I can watch over you from the other side, then I shall certainly do so.

Bless you.

Father

This fifty-four-year-old businessman died of an overdose of prescription drugs. His textiles business was on the verge of bankruptcy. Six months previously he had stopped maintenance payments to his wife, from whom he was separated. His family doctor told the police that his deceased patient had been suffering from high blood pressure and circulation problems for years, and that he had added serious kidney disease to his list of ailments in recent weeks.

32

To all my dear darlings,

Here's a final goodbye to all of you from Dad / Father-in-law / Grandpa.

I expect you are all very sad now. There you are sitting around the table, and there's an empty chair. But that's only how it seems on the outside. I'm still there – in you and through you. Don't hang your heads. That's the way life is, that's the way of the world. As I write these lines today, I'm not remotely thinking about dying, and I hope that it will still be a while, but it often happens more quickly than you think.

My dear G,

Well, I did go before you after all – how many times did I say I wanted it to happen this way?! That wasn't egotism, but a desire that you should enjoy all them lovely things we worked for more than I ever did.

Life goes on, and life's our children who all really do need their Mum and Gran now, so chin up Mum

I want to use this moment when you're all sitting together, or so I hope, to thank you again Mum for all the lovely hours you've given me. Right to the very end you've been a true and dearly loved friend, a lovely wife and good friend, and if I could start my life all over again, it'd only ever be with you, it was lovely by your side, and even on miserable days I could see the sun rising on the horizon if I was by your side.

I'd most certainly live my life the way I led it this time, maybe with one change — I'd leave out the worry and suffering I sometimes caused you Mum.

Police detectives initially suspected an accident when they discovered the body of fifty-year-old EZ in a courtyard. EZ had been drinking with colleagues the previous evening, though nothing unusual appeared to have happened. He had been cheerful during the evening, had gone to bed at around 11 p.m., and had fallen out of the window an hour later. The seven-metre fall had broken his spine and smashed his skull. His watch had stopped at two minutes past midnight.

During the investigation, however, an accident started to seem increasingly unlikely. EZ had only drunk two bottles of beer and four vodkas, so he was by no means blind drunk. There was evidence that he had climbed onto a desk in front of a window in order to open it and jump out. Furthermore, his briefcase contained a suicide note, 'the second part of which may not have been written until the night concerned'.

EZ was the father of four children and had only just celebrated his silver wedding anniversary. The family's finances were in good order and Z had no debts. In the early 1960s he had been sent on a course that he had to abandon early because his work was not up to standard. In conversations with acquaintances, Z said that his self-confidence had suffered tremendously and that he had never got over this blow. When relatives and colleagues were questioned, however, there was no evidence of serious conflicts or problems. His achievements at work were undisputed; only a few days earlier he had received a bonus. EZ's superior emphasised that he had 'scored a number of successes at work, especially recently'.

His doctor, however, stated that he had treated EZ for 'persistent symptoms of stress', and that he had frequently taken tranquillisers. His wife also referred to his restlessness and sleeplessness, particularly after consuming even small quantities of alcohol. EZ had also had a 'strong reaction' to mixing alcohol and valium in the past. Investigators therefore concluded that he 'could have acted in a manner beyond his control' during that fatal night. The final report by the police contained the brief statement: 'Motive: illness'.

33

15 March

My dear loved ones,

I've spent ages wondering whether I should write or not. And that's because the more I think about it, the more difficult it is to maintain any hope of ever being understood. All the same I'm going to try to express my ever more intense thoughts and feelings in this form. In any case, this is the only form I have left. Difficult though the decision was, I've chosen to take my own life. What has brought me to this?

1.) The fact – which I find dreadful – that I'm suffering from a disease that, according to the doctors, can return at any moment without my being able to do anything about it. Even the 'art of medicine' is currently still not capable of treating the causes; all it can do is minimise the symptoms. For someone who works with the mind, as I do, this illness [manic depression] with all its symptoms is on a par with a manual worker losing a hand. I don't want to re-live everything I have experienced and lived through during the past year. I realise more and more *that something inside me has snapped; something that won't ever grow back together again. I know I'm not the same person I was a year ago, and I don't believe I'll ever be able to create anything with such élan ever again.*

2.) Although I've made an effort to create something during this period, I have to be honest and admit that, because of this illness, it's partly been wrong, and in many cases just fragmentary bits and pieces. That's never happened to me before – so it has to be a side-effect of this disease and its treatment. Maybe the doctors still aren't aware of this, but the two doses of electric shock therapy that I underwent didn't just give me a crippled right leg but in my opinion also engendered bad side-effects in my thought-processes, such as an inability to concentrate. In particular, I used to be able to reason my way through a plethora of facts and unfailingly arrive at a fresh conclusion – but not any more.

3.) The 'expert opinion' regarding my pension application branded me a defective person. But I don't want to receive charity!

4.) The idea that when the children are a bit older they would be able to visit their father in a lunatic asylum.

5.) The chance that this might be genetic, that B and I are already condemned to this, and that it might manifest itself one day. The very thought of this is in itself unbearable.

6.) *The fact that we thought that I'd got over the illness, only to find the opposite was true, largely as a result of the doctors' advice – no doubt well meant – to take on a light job initially.*

But what was really going on? I had thought that I'd be able to keep my former job, and that I'd gradually regain my self-confidence – if I were somewhat away from the front-line. Instead, I was told that they didn't want to take the risk – and that, coming from friends to whom I'd selflessly devoted all my knowledge and all my skills!

Instead, I was offered a 'light job', namely two posts as departmental manager responsible for rationalisation and automation – one in a big plant, the other in a planning office. So in fact these were major tasks, on top of which the departments first had to be built up, quite apart from working in a strange environment. I see that as being pushed out.

'The Moor has done his duty . . .' Then that led to my desperate attempt to commit suicide by overdosing on tablets. Unfortunately it didn't work, and I ended up back in two madhouses. The second time in hospital was thanks to E.

7.) *There's no doubt that E coped very bravely with that particular year – I don't know whether I'd have been able to do so. All the same, my illness – viewed in the sober light of day – is a real burden on my family.*

I sense quite clearly that with the passage of time a barrier is steadily building up between E and me and between the children and me, a barrier that allows us to peep through only very occasionally, and then only out of pity.

I can't any longer tell E the kinds of thoughts I'm writing here, for fear of being sent back to hospital as 'relapsed'. I don't want that kind of dependency.

8.) And finally there's the uncertainty about the financial situation, which has already been going on for four months now. Just imagine: interim payments of 75 per month for me, and 40 per month for each child. I'd like to see anyone live on that.

I expect the problem of providing for the surviving members of the family will be sorted out more quickly with a death certificate than with a birth certificate.

What with all I've described above, there is very little pleasure for me in being alive. The dreadful things I've experienced in the last year, the unsatisfactory present and the dark future – these things all lead yet again to increasing insomnia, senseless brooding etc. That's not living, it's just vegetating.

When everything's done and dusted – I hope it works, and that I'm spared a third trip to the madhouse – I'm quite sure that all your lives will soon revert to normal, and that what you've experienced will seem like nothing more than a bad dream. I'm sorry to have to put you through the pain, but at the end of the day, everyone must know for himself when his time has come.

I'm hoping for peace at last – peace, peace, and more peace. Saying goodbye is easier because I don't believe in a beyond.

I'd so much like to have done more, especially for the children – but it clearly wasn't to be.

Finally, I'd like to thank you for all the kind things you have done for me.

However you view and judge my actions – one thing's for sure – it can't be objective, because you're not in my shoes.

Better a terrible end than terror without end.

Take care

R

RW, a thirty-four-year-old government ministry employee, was always full of ideas, and often worked way beyond his contracted hours; however, he suddenly attracted attention when he started coming out with confused remarks. Very soon after his admission to a psychiatric hospital, the doctor treating him forecast that 'to judge by my experiences with other patients, he will kill himself after a couple of years'. Contrary to this prognosis, the recovery initially proceeded at great speed, and the patient was released. Then, however, he had a relapse. Even imported drugs made no difference; nor did the electric shock treatment that the doctors resorted to. An improvement could be discerned only very gradually, and when he was finally released from the mental hospital the prognosis was that 'his mental state of health will continue to oscillate between highs and lows'.

This being the case, the ministry no longer wanted him to work for them; he asked if he could take a job as a college lecturer or professor, but his request was rejected as pie in the sky. He was offered three departmental managerial posts, whereupon he attempted suicide.

Following this, the ministry initiated the procedure for retirement on medical grounds. He was notified about pension arrangements, but the money wasn't initially forthcoming because a signature was missing. This problem was sorted out the following January; the pension was to be paid retrospectively, and, according to information provided by the insurance office, he was informed of this by telephone. The pension was to be quite generous. A formal assessment at his place of work described him as an outstanding worker, displaying extraordinary strength of will, discipline and commitment.

A highly qualified engineer, RW demonstrated his talent for technological invention even in his final moments. He ran a hose from the gas stove in the kitchen through to the sitting room. There he lay on the sofa and pulled a plastic bag over his head (secured around his neck) with the end of the hose inside it. He ran a second hose from the plastic bag onto the balcony so that the gas could escape into the fresh air. Police investigators concluded that he had done this in order to prevent an explosion, which might otherwise have occurred when someone else came into the flat.

34

Dear parents, brother and sisters,

I'd like to send you another couple of lines today. I just wanted to let you know that after the three years I still won't be let out. I've only just found out the reason. The courts decided that after my jail I should be forced into a sycyatree to be Curred, but Im not ill. So Ive had a think about my life and Ive also realised that my life could of been diffrent if Id listened to you sometimes when I was 14, but I always had big ideas and wanted to be Grown up, but I know now myself that you were sometimes right after all. Youll probbly think Im just trying to impress you or make you feel sorry for me, but thats not trew. The thing is Im totally fed up with life. and if I dont get threw these 3 years then them outside can at least say I was sorry for what I done and realised what mistakes Id made. Dad your perhaps the only one who knows what things have been like for me sometimes. Your words have sometimes given me extra courage but I Thought being grown up would be easier. Now Id like to be back with you all again. Dad please tell my brother and sisters how things are with me menterly and morally my nerves are shot to hell. Ive completely changed. if you *seed me youd be horrified. My hands shake when I smoke a cigarette. i cant sleep properly at night either. Dad what you wrote in your last letter that I should look into myself for my mistakes is what made me realise these things.*

And please tell my 3 sisters that I want to say sorry for all the stuff I've dumped on them throughout their life. Ive always been very fond of Them all and that's why it was a big shock when I came home and theyd all gone there own ways and it wasnt like it was when I left home. Ive always been very fond of my brother M too and I think he was fond of me too. Dad Im very fond of you and Mum and dont want to loose you but life don't give me no pleasure any more.

So thats why I want to end it here, dont let your lives be ruined, theres one less of you to worry about now.

Bye, youre son and brother

S

By the time he died, twenty-five-year-old S had already spent several years of his young life in jail. He was imprisoned for sexually abusing children, and then again for coercion and sexual abuse. In prison he attracted attention because of his rebelliousness and readiness to use violence, and according to the prison officer in charge of him was deemed unwilling to improve his behaviour. On 3 August he was put in a punishment cell for hitting another prisoner. There, he twisted his vest into a noose, tied it to the bars of the window, and hanged himself.

Only afterwards was it discovered that S had formulated a suicide note the day before. The highly eccentric spelling (for instance, 'sycyatree' means 'psychiatry') is no reflection on him. As he was unable to read and write, he dictated the letter to a fellow inmate.

35

Please pass on my warm regards

to everyone listed below. I'd like to ask this question: what's the meaning of humankind (in the universal scheme of things)?? Is it to be a destroyer? None exists.

C, a twenty-year-old lance-corporal, offers a prime example of something that is quite common among young people: their farewell lines don't shed any light on the reasons behind their suicide but, rather, obscure them. On the evening of 29 January, while doing sentry duty on his own near the assault course, C killed himself with a bullet through the head. He was still alive when he was found, but died shortly afterwards in hospital.

His last few words, which he'd scribbled down in his pocket diary, left everyone baffled. His personal files contained 'no previous convictions, no personal peculiarities'. Everyone in the young soldier's circle was questioned, but nobody could even begin to offer an explanation, and nobody had reckoned on him committing suicide. One soldier merely remembered having overheard a conversation a long time before. During this

144

conversation, a soldier whom he didn't know had said to C that he'd never have the courage to turn a weapon on himself. C had retorted: 'You'll see.'

Income	156.00
Rent	43.65
Light	12.60
Laundry	15.00
Grave	10.00
Coal	5.00
Debts	8.00
156.00	
94.25	
61.75	

You can't live and smoke for 31 days on 61.75, so have a good time then end it.

This 'balance sheet' was drawn up by a fifty-eight-year-old man who took his own life. He was on an invalidity pension, had started drinking after the death of his wife, and was constantly in debt.

Dear loved ones

Please don't be angry with me if I don't wake up again. It really is the best thing for me. When you're in such pain day and night, it's not a life any more. The pains have been getting worse by the day, I couldn't even go shopping in town any more. Being alive is nothing but torture now. Please forgive me, and remember me fondly.

With a heavy heart

Your mother

This pensioner lived in an area with an above-average suicide rate, where 42 per cent of suicides lived in isolation and the majority of them were pensioners.

38

Thank you for your efforts.

Take care. Don't forget your Granny, U. G, you always took pity on me when I was in bed. B just lets me lie there like a child, without food and drink or even so much as a word. Other than that, she was good and hard-working. I was ill, very very ill.

While her daughter-in-law was briefly out of the house this fifty-seven-year-old woman turned on all four gas burners on her stove. She had been treated for years for cerebral arteriosclerosis and diabetes. In her case, the diagnosis was 'increasing mental deterioration to the point of apathy'.

Interhotel C, 1.11

To the police, or the doctor responsible for issuing the death certificate.

1. Personal details

Dr G

2. Facts of the case

Suicide (sleeping tablet overdose) using

42.5g Kalypnon

26.0g Cyclobarbital

4.0g Lepinal

This should far exceed the survival threshold for a 30g dose of barbiturates as described by the pharmacologist Hauschild and others.

3. *Motive*

There is a motive.

4. I should like to ask that an autopsy not be carried out on my body if at all possible, since I . . . too worked in forensic medicine and had to witness too many colleagues in all the various institutions who would sooner. . ., but that would 'probably' be an insult to many of my former colleagues.

A fatal dose of barbiturates in the bloodstream can easily be detected by simple vein and heart. . . – and this method is practised in B too.

If a post-mortem is mandatory in the circumstances, then please entrust the task to Dr [. . .]. I would ask her as a friend to do me this last favour <u>here in C</u> and to keep it strictly to herself.

Dr G

PS I would ask that my bosses and all other inquisitive persons be told that the finding was 'injuries pursuant to a road accident'.

R,

Right by the hotel you'll find the car and the cats – still alive, I hope! – plus the suitcase and, inside it, the missing jewellery box. Please forgive me, and please try to understand. Do you still remember that incredibly clever Mexican saying about marriage? How true it was – and how dearly I loved you!

Your E

Dear R,

Forgive me for what's happened. Please tell <u>everyone</u> it was a <u>road accident</u>. They'll believe you, it being November, foggy, and 'my style of driving'. I chose C so that hopefully everything can be sorted out with complete discretion.

Why did you leave me on my own?

I'm going – I'm unimaginably calm and collected. I so longed for a happy way out together <u>with you</u>, and so long as I had the strength I tried hard to achieve it!!

For my daughters J and N in remembrance of their mother. [pearl earrings were attached to the letter at this point]

I'm giving you, dear R, my bracelet (that I always loved wearing) in remembrance of a woman who loved you infinitely, and whom you understood so little. [a two-piece bracelet was attached to the letter here]

'Good luck, and all the best'

Your wife

My dear R,

Please try to understand the changes to my will – some of them very tough – but . . . from my Aunt . . .'s will compel me to return the rings we've come to love (otherwise, they'd end up going to . . .!!) But I hope you'll be able to sort things out financially with . . . by [further, almost illegible, details from the will follow here].

As you know, I was always a bit 'crazy' as you called it. All the same, I think a lovely ceramic box, or a ceramic pot, is a lot more attractive than a black standard-issue urn! In loving memory, and longing for a last hug, a kiss, I'll say goodbye – for ever. I chose 'freedom' and ask for my dog and, should you get rid of the cats, for . . ..

I wish you 'good luck and all the best' for a better future from the bottom of my heart.

You're the only one I ever truly loved!!

Your wife.

The washing still has to be taken to the . . . If I don't sell any kittens at the show, then my bank account will be in the red again . . .

EG, a doctor, had gone to C for a pedigree cat show. It was Sunday morning when a hotel employee found her dead on the floor of her hotel room. Dr G had written an 'official' suicide note in bureaucratic form, listing among other things the lethal cocktail of drugs she had taken. An empty water tumbler with a whitish residue stood next to the letter.

She had parked her car in front of the hotel. There, several further suicide notes to her husband were found, along with the cats; the notes are almost illegible in parts. Pieces of jewellery were attached to one of the letters.

As the motive wasn't clearly identifiable from the letters, her husband was questioned. He stated that his wife had suffered from depressive moods previously. Two years earlier, she had attempted to hang herself after failing an examination. Although she re-sat and passed the examination and, after a long search, found a job, she remained pessimistic and had her will notarised. According to her husband, their marriage had not currently been in crisis.

Dr G went to C with seven pedigree cats. Following a veterinary examination, her stud cat (on which her registered stud entirely depended) was declared unsuitable for breeding. According to the final police report, several breeders had avoided Dr G during the cat show because she had seemed highly distracted and unfocused.

40

01.04.1987

Explanation

There's only – one – explanation for my actions: drunk at the wheel.

Not really a plausible reason.

But enough of a reason for someone who failed shamefully in front of his friends and in his own eyes (despite knowing better).

My car's on the right at the main entrance.

On 31 March 1978, thirty-seven-year-old Z, an army officer, was sitting with his friends in a bar. He drank approximately five brandies and a bottle of beer, then got in his car and drove home. The police stopped him shortly after 11 p.m. near the local police station, arrested him for driving under the influence of alcohol, and confiscated his driving licence.

Three hours later Z returned to his flat, said hello to his wife and told her he had to go out again straight away. He went to the bathroom, had a wash, pocketed an apple, and set off. The wife assumed that there was some kind of emergency along the border. She looked out of the window again and watched her husband drive off in his car.

It was not yet 6 a.m. when Z got to work. He parked his car in the street and went to his office. Sometime between six and seven o'clock, he shot himself.

When interviewed, Z's colleagues described him as an ambitious and over-zealous officer. He was, they said, highly sensitive whenever his own behaviour or personality was in the spotlight. They believed – and his wife agreed – that he acted as he did 'due to a misplaced sense of honour and a feeling of shame at his own responsibility'. There were no grounds for alternative explanations (such as accident or murder). There was also no suggestion of any other misdemeanours. The officer's files proved to be complete and in order. The police checked that the suicide note was genuine, but the only oddity was the fact that Z had written the wrong date (1987 instead of 1978). It was presumably a case of 'confusion caused by agitation'.

41

Inspection of the flat 9.15am/ 23.06

1) Typed letter with black border: 'To quote your own words: you don't need to kiss my arse any more!'

(Passport photo of a woman pinned to it)

Letter attached to a nail in the wall opposite the front door

2) Floor of the hall: sheet of squared A4 paper: 'These lines to the court. . .'; sunglasses next to it.

Mirror (with brown resin paint): 'How pretty you were'

<u>Bedroom</u>

Double bed against outside wall

Left wall: wardrobe with 5 doors

with 'All the BEST' written in brown resin paint above the doors

Wall opposite the double bed:

Poster depicting alpine landscape

written on it with brown resin paint:

'Once this too was meant to symbolise harmony!
Unfortunately'

– to the right, mirrored console > mirror broken

– console doors broken

– shelf above double bed smeared with oily fluid

– Duvets cut up; contents (feathers) spilt out

– on mirrored console, empty litre bottle labelled
'Graphite Oil'

<u>*Bathroom*</u>

Electrical equipment in the bathtub (full of water)

– vacuum cleaner

– stereo system

– barbecue

■ Let Me Finish

– *tape recorder*

– *food mixer*

– *coffee machine*

– *toaster*

– *drill*

Cupboard above washing machine (doors ripped off)

[a list of medicines followed here]

Wall above bathtub: 'Enjoy the feeling'

Wall by door: 'I'm not sorry'

<u>*Kitchen*</u>

Left-hand sink

Remnants of a blue index card

burnt / 1 match

Freezer: meat / fruit / vegetables

– *door open; unplugged*

– *on the outside: brown heart smeared over it*

Living room

– *colour TV destroyed (tube)*

– *wall cupboards > doors torn off, smashed with axe or similar*

– *paint daubs on wall cupboards*

– *flower pots / crockery smashed*

– *suite of furniture slashed / covered in paint*

– *paint-like substance on carpets and rugs*

– *fragments of crystal decanter and glasses*

Children's room

– *no damage*

– *bunk bed with note attached to edge of ladder on top bunk (squared A4)*

> *we want to be buried together*

Balcony

left and right: blinds attached to a pole with rings, unpicked towards the bottom

Flower boxes on balcony rail > flowers mostly cut off or torn out

At midday on 22 June, thirty-two-year-old RS rang his wife at her work to say goodbye to her 'for ever'. The couple had been divorced the previous day. The wife was awarded custody of the children aged seven and ten.

As he himself admitted, S had been keen to obtain a divorce for years. Shortly before his death, he made a tape recording in which he said it was because he considered his wife to be incapable of bringing the children up properly.

He had threatened to 'do something about it' if she were given custody following the divorce. This is what had now happened.

After smashing up the flat, RS collected his two children from school. He put his foot down on the motorway and rammed his car into a bridge pillar at full speed. The car immediately caught fire; RS had put two cans full of petrol in the boot before setting off, and had left the caps off.

A work colleague described RS as a 'truth fanatic with a strong sense of justice, who could talk extremely eloquently, at length, and in detail about even trivial things'. She described his manner as uncontrolled and totalitarian. For him there were no nuances or shades of grey, she said; everything always had to be black or white.

By the time you receive this letter

I'll be dead. (It's an imposition, I know, but I can't think of anyone else to turn to.) I'm not going to try to justify something that's unjustifiable; it's absurd and incomprehensible enough compared to 'life'.

I'd 'had it with life' for a long time; the idea of ending my own life as a last resort has been familiar to me for years now: the more I realised my powerlessness and inability to live the life I wanted to live, the more the notion grew of my ultimate restrictedness and the way I could 'get rid' of it: since I couldn't live (whatever 'living' might be) I wanted at least to die. (Absurd enough, but it's difficult to find the right language and the right images.)

All the respect and solidarity that I encountered during the last month and at your house, and to such a high degree; this feeling that had lain buried for years, that I didn't believe existed for me any more, this indescribably beautiful sense of being humanly safe and secure, spread out right across my broken inner self –

So much so that it's now difficult to say adieu.

Essentially I'm 'sick of it': sick of this country and its rules; sick of this society, of this socialism that isn't socialism; of the police, and of the all-pervading fear that you feel as soon as you diverge from the normal, well-trodden path. Every deviation seems lethal; I've had enough of it, but above all I've had enough of myself, too: my silence, my coldness, my well-established conformism.

I made a definite mistake during my time in the army when I passed up the opportunity to change countries without any risk. I don't know if it would have done me any good, but you can die anywhere when all's said and done – not much consolation, but even so.

I know what I don't want any more. I don't want to wear a uniform ever again; I'd rather die myself than have to train and practise killing people. I don't want to live without love – in however meagre a form – any more. I don't want to be confronted by my fear and depressive weakness any more, the ever-increasing paralysis that makes me apathetic and cynical. I don't want to be just a loser any more or watch myself disintegrate psychologically knowing I don't have the strength to change. (This is turning into an orgy of justification all by itself, but this is the last thing I want it to be.)

I shall die; I know that my death will hurt a few people,

and that their hurt won't heal easily, especially not my parents'. (I would very much like to ask your forgiveness – but there's no forgiveness for this sort of thing, just as there are no convincing explanations that anyone could follow through in their own mind, as this letter clearly demonstrates.)

To all who were fond of me I should like to say: don't be sad, forget me quickly, forgetting helps, and anyway I've just gone on a bit ahead of you, that's all. Goodbye, then, and thanks for everything.

[blacked out signature]

My last request: that this letter be made accessible to my parents above all (. . .) and . . ., as well as . . . No death announcements in the newspaper; a quiet and simple funeral. My body is to be cremated.

Books, records and suchlike that I've given or lent to people are to be kept by them.

[blacked out signature]

PS The key to the flat is in the letter box, which is open.

Little is known about this young advertising designer who killed himself. He was in his early twenties and wrote poems, some of which were astonishingly good – so much so that friends were planning to publish them in book form. An author was going to write a treatise on them as he regarded the young poet as 'a rare case of someone who leaves behind writings that express all the contradictions of today's young people and of their life, thought and language'. However, nothing came of this.

43

My dear sparrow,

You were so good to me and wanted me to become healthy. But I realise that things are going further and further downhill with me and that I can't think clearly any more. I want to spare you, the children and myself from having to spend the rest of my life in a madhouse.

It wouldn't make you happy any more than it would me.

So don't begrudge me my peace. Life is just torture for me.

Thank you for the last lovely hours and generally for everything you've done for me.

I hope my children don't suffer the same illness and that they grow up to be good, solid citizens.

I'd love to have stayed with you, but in my condition I'm no use to you or the country.

I'd like to write more, but my memory has forsaken me completely.

With love,

Your sparrow

A thousand kisses to my children and my good parents, and to Aunt E, Uncle H, A and K.

Severe headaches and mental stress had made life unbearable for this qualified shorthand-typist and mother of two. She was restless, couldn't sleep at night, and regularly suffered from excruciating headaches. She had been treated as an in-patient eighteen months before her death. The doctors established that her symptoms were not caused by any organic problem, and sent her home again three weeks later. She experienced a short-term improvement in her condition before the same symptoms reappeared.

There were evidently no problems in her private life. The suicide note was written just before she made an attempt to kill herself with an overdose of tablets. However, she was rescued and came home from hospital in good physical health. After a last weekend with her family, she hanged herself.

44

I've come back because

I'm feeling worse and worse. Yes, I can sleep now thanks
to the tablets, but during the day I'm just as I was before,
and I've got all sorts of twitches so that I can't work
properly any more.

Since I imagine there's no way for me to get out of this
hopeless situation I've now got to the stage of thinking
about suicide.

Very depressed that I'm reacting so badly to these difficul-
ties when they're only to do with work, and that these
crises keep returning. Feel I've failed in life (job and
other people), indecision,

<u>High points</u>

Times of great confidence, can't keep my mouth shut,
often the life and soul of the party.

Highly eloquent, previous career successes

Crisis points

1st crisis: separation from family, very difficult to start with

2nd and 3rd crisis: problems at work, times of great insecurity. Have barely any contact with other people, don't talk much, don't have anyone. . . [final two words illegible].

On 8 September the body of an engineer, who had disappeared a week earlier, was found by the police in woodland. The twenty-eight-year-old had been undergoing psychiatric treatment for manic depression for a considerable time. Shortly before his death he believed that he had made an important discovery. This resulted in an angry dispute with his head of department, who advised him against being over-hasty in publishing his results and told him to do further experiments to substantiate his bold hypothesis. It finally transpired that the departmental head's reservations were justified, as the original hypothesis could not in fact be proved correct. The engineer's euphoric mood swiftly evaporated. He was already seriously suicidal by the end of August; he set off with a net full of stones, intending to throw himself and the net into a lake. He'd had a doctor's appointment the day he disappeared. The neurologist told him that he couldn't help him either at that point, and that he was to keep on taking the tablets.

45

Things for K-U in your car

Now I'll manage it Love you but my life is over now. Thanks for your strange love don't get it take care.

In 2001, the first case of a suicide note via text message was published. The text message was left by a thirty-four-year-old man, whose partner described him as hysterical, unstable and bad tempered. They had fought several times in the past. During a particularly fierce row, he threatened to take his own life and the woman left the flat. An hour later she received the text message on her mobile phone, entered the flat with two acquaintances, and discovered that her boyfriend had hanged himself.

Selected References

Introduction

Jean Améry, *On Suicide: A Discourse on Voluntary Death*, Bloomington, 1999.

Jean Baechler, *Suicides*, New York 1979.

Hermann Burger, *Tractatus logico-suicidalis*, Frankfurt am Main, 1988.

Gabriele Dietze (ed.) *Todeszeichen: Freitod in Selbstzeugnissen*, Frankfurt am Main, 1981.

Wilhelm Kamlah, *Meditatio mortis*, Stuttgart, 1976.

Peter Loosen, 'Untersuchungen an Selbstmörderabschiedsbriefen', Dissertation Düsseldorf 1969.

W. Morgenthaler, *Letzte Aufzeichnungen von Selbstmördern*, Berne, 1945.

www.samaritans.org

Roger Willemsen (ed.), *Der Selbstmord in Berichten, Briefen, Manifesten, Dokumenten und literarischen Texten* (Munich, 2003).

Letters

The letters that appear in this book, and the research that the author undertook, were all originally in German. Full details are given here of those originals, for any reader wanting to refer to them.

1 BstU, MfS, BV Halle, Abt.IX, Nr.217.

2 Helmut Kulawik/Dieter Decke, 'Letze Aufzeich-nungen – eine Analyse von 223 nach vollendeten Suiziden hinterlassenen Briefen und Mitteilungen' in: *Psychiatrica clinica* 6 (1973) S.193-210, zit.197f.

3 STAL, BdVP Leipzig, 24.1, Nr.2437.

4 Irma Schierl, 'Suizide in ländlichen Gebieten, Klein- und Mittelstädten', Dissertation Erlangen-Nürnberg 1973, S.109.

5 Peter Loosen, 'Untersuchungen an Selbstmörder-abschiedsbriefen', Dissertation Düsseldorf 1969, Anhang Nr.27.

6 STAL, BdVP Leipzig, 24.1, Nr.2953.

7 BStU, MfS, AS 105/72, Bd.1, Bl.100-105.

8 'Frequently dreaming about a deceased spouse is in itself a normal part of the widowed person's psycho-logical reaction to grief,' wrote Wolfgang Döhner in a 1984 dissertation in which this letter was published. According to him, the case quoted here shows that 'such dreams can, however, resemble suicide fantasies and take on a strong allure'. Wolfgang Döhner, 'Suizid nach Partnerverlust durch Verwitwung oder

Scheidung', Dissertation Heidelberg 1984, S.105f.

9 BStU, MfS, BV Halle, Abt.IX, Nr.642, Bl.395f.

10 Peter Loosen, 'Untersuchungen an Selbstmörder-abschiedsbriefen', Dissertation Düsseldorf 1969, Anhang Nr.18.

11 BStU, MfS, AS 290/71, Bl.122-125.

12 Sächs. HStA Dresden, BdVP Dresden (MUK), Nr.114.

13 BStU, MfS, BV Halle, Abt.IX, Nr.17.

14 The author of this dissertation, who was training to be a psychiatrist, wrote by way of introduction: 'Several letters by young people, all written shortly before they were seventeen, have various characteristics in common, all of them typical of people going through puberty: pompous, cliché-ridden expressions assuming an air of experience and precociousness, all of them revolving around the idea of searching for the meaning and point of life. Thus we find statements of an almost poetic nature alongside philosophising observations. For example, one schoolboy of 16 years and 6 months begins his lengthy expostulations as follows: . . .' This is followed by the poem quoted. Friedemann Ficker, 'Suizidale Handlungen in Kindheit und Pubertät', Dissertation Dresden 1977, S.89.

15 StAC, BT/RdB Karl-Marx-Stadt, Abt. Volksbildung, Nr.057850, n.pag.

16 STAL, BdVP Leipzig, 24.1, Nr.2950.

17 These extracts were published in a medical dissertation in 1977. The second letter was published only

in summary form. Friedemann Ficker, 'Suizidale Handlungen in Kindheit und Pubertät', Dissertation Dresden 1977, S.89f.

18 This (slightly abridged) suicide note was published in a textbook by a teacher from Kiel. Gerhild Heuer, *Selbstmord bei Kindern und Jugendlichen*, Stuttgart 1979, S.92.

19 BStU, MfS, BV Halle, Abt.IX, Nr.308.

20 *Informationsdienst Telefonseelsorge*, Heft 6, Mai 1978, S.18-21.

21 StAC, BT/RdB Karl-Marx-Stadt, Abt. Volksbildung, Nr.102173, n.pag.

22 StAC, BT/RdB Karl-Marx-Stadt, Abt. Volksbildung, Nr.057846, n.pag.

23 'Seafaring was presumably not how R had expected it to be. He was clearly miserable about the fact that his boat hadn't docked anywhere for a long while,' wrote Wolfgang Wodarg, who quoted the suicide note of the young seaman in a 1979 dissertation. Wodarg eliminated other motives such as love problems, problems with his parents, seasickness or alcohol abuse. R had not apparently been teased by the other sailors. He was said to have drawn little attention to himself, shown unfailing helpfulness, and got on well with everyone. Wolfgang Wodarg, 'Psychische Krankheiten der Seeleute', Dissertation Rehburg-Loccum 1979, S.18f.

24 BLHA Potsdam, BdVP Potsdam, Rep.404/15.2, Nr.1284.

25 This letter was published in a dissertation in 1973.

The author, a doctor, offered it as an example of psychosis as the motivating factor behind suicide. However, she did say that she had merely picked out one isolated symptom that suggested schizophrenia or paranoid psychosis with hallucinations, and admitted that 'The subtle structure of her insanity could only have been properly described by examining the sick woman herself.' Irma Schierl, 'Suizide in ländlichen Gebieten, Klein- und Mittelstädten', Dissertation Erlangen-Nürnberg 1973, S.82.

26 BStU, MfS, HA VII, Nr.1025, Bl.101-103.

27 BStU, MfS, HA IX, Nr.10758, Bl.19-21.

28 STAL, BdVP Leipzig, 24.1, Nr.2355.

29 BStU, MfS, AS 304/71, Bl.25-31.

30 BStU, MfS, AS 105/72, Bl.147f.

31 BStU, MfS, HA I, Nr.11175, Bl.25f.

32 BStU, MfS, HA I, Nr.20, Bl.569-574.

33 Peter Loosen, 'Untersuchungen an Selbstmörder abschiedsbriefen', Dissertation Düsseldorf 1969, Anhang Nr.75.

34 BStU, MfS, AS 16/74, Bl.18f.

35 STAL, BdVP Leipzig, 24.1, Nr.2435.

36 Peter Loosen, 'Untersuchungen an Selbstmörder-abschiedsbriefen', Dissertation Düsseldorf 1969, Anhang Nr.38.

37 A trainee doctor who analysed the situation in his dissertation discovered that this region had been seriously affected by brown coal mining. The author of the dissertation did not succeed in speaking to the relatives of any of those who had died. Ulf Warstat,

'Untersuchungen der Suizide eines Landkreises im Zeitraum 1980-89 und Betrachtungen zur Suizid-prophylaxe', Dissertation Halle/Saale 1992, S.25.

38 BStU, MfS, BV Halle, Abt.IX, Nr.46.
39 BStU, MfS, AS 105/72, Bl.298-305.
40 BStU, MfS, AS 30/77, Bl.19.
41 BStU, MfS, HA IX, Nr.10758, Bl.3-17.
42 BStU, MfS, AIM 7423/91, Bd.6, Bl.90f.
43 BStU, MfS, AS 152/74, Bl.439.
44 BLHA, Rep.530, SED-BL Potsdam, Nr.3360, Bl.59.
45 This case was published in the *Medical Tribune* by forensic scientists from Berlin. Adieu per SMS. 'Selbstmörder mailte Abschiedsbrief', in: *Medical Tribune*, Ausgabe 18/2002, S.28.